PAPER BLOOMS

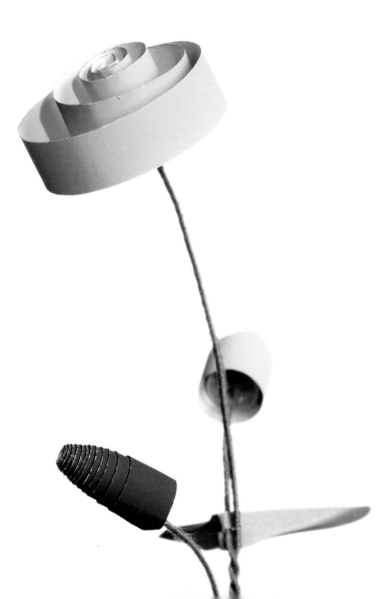

PAPER BLOOMS

25 Extraordinary Flowers to Make
for Weddings, Celebrations & More

Jeffery Rudell

LARK CRAFTS
Asheville

An Imprint of Sterling Publishing
387 Park Avenue South
New York, NY 10016

© 2013 by Jeffery Rudell

ISBN 978-1-4547-0350-1

Library of Congress Cataloging-in-Publication Data

Rudell, Jeffery.
    Paper blooms : 25 extraordinary flowers to make for weddings,
celebrations & more / Jeffery Rudell. -- First Edition.
       pages cm
    Includes index.
    ISBN 978-1-4547-0350-1
    1. Paper flowers. I. Title.
    TT892.R83 2013
    745.594'3--dc23
                                               2012015224

Distributed in Canada by Sterling Publishing
c/o Canadian Manda Group, 165 Dufferin Street
Toronto, Ontario, Canada M6K 3H6
Distributed in the United Kingdom by GMC Distribution Services
Castle Place, 166 High Street, Lewes, East Sussex, England BN7 1XU
Distributed in Australia by Capricorn Link (Australia) Pty. Ltd.
P.O. Box 704, Windsor, NSW 2756, Australia

For information about custom editions, special sales, and premium and corporate purchases, please contact
Sterling Special Sales at 800-805-5489 or specialsales@sterlingpublishing.com.

Email academic@larkbooks.com for information about desk and examination copies.
The complete policy can be found at larkcrafts.com.

Every effort has been made to ensure that all the information in this book is accurate. However, due to
differing conditions, tools, and individual skills, the publisher cannot be responsible for any injuries, losses,
and other damages that may result from the use of the information in this book.

Manufactured in China

2 4 6 8 10 9 7 5 3 1

larkcrafts.com

contents

Flowers: we are continually drawn to them, lured by their elegance, beauty, structure, and form. There is something special about a perfect flower—the delicate bend of a stem, or a flush of color—that never fails to add a little cheer to the day.

The evocative quality of real flowers can also be created with paper flowers. With this book as your guide, the process is not only possible, but easy. Placed in a vase to brighten a room, wrapped in tissue paper and given as a gift, or combined in a bouquet to be carried down an aisle by a bride, paper flowers are both a tasteful accent and a thoughtful gesture. Whether imbued with traditional meaning or accompanied by a thoughtful note, paper flowers are the perfect way to express yourself.

In this book I offer you a wealth of seasonal floral options to suit every occasion. Each flower design retains the handmade look that is the hallmark of the best crafts, while reflecting the sophistication that is the mark of good design.

Paper flowers, like the live blooms they mimic, are temporary; they are not meant to last forever. But if made using reasonably good paper stock and reliable glue, they will remain fresh and beautiful for many years to come.

I invite you to discover the creative world of paper flowers.

The Simple Basics of Making Paper Flowers

CUT, FOLD, GLUE—EASY

The skills needed to create the projects featured in this book are very simple. Many of them you may have learned years ago, including how to handle a craft knife, a pair of scissors, and a hot glue gun. In addition, some common paper-specific maneuvers will prove helpful, namely: folding, curling, shaping, and gluing. For anyone unfamiliar with any of these (or if you find yourself a little out of practice), I recommend beginning with the projects near the front of the book until you feel confident in your abilities. The projects are grouped by paper-cutting technique (strips of paper, paper punches, and hand-cut paper) and become a little more challenging the further along you go, with the skills required for the later projects building upon those featured earlier in the book.

That being said, if you are like me, you will likely ignore the table of contents and simply begin with whichever flower is your favorite.

In truth, the skill most required throughout this book is simple patience—with yourself as you learn something new, and with your material as you explore its possibilities and limitations. While some of these flower designs can be created quickly and with minimal effort, others demand a little more time to complete, and a few require a substantial investment of time. In many ways, these projects are like knitting, crocheting, and quilting in that a lot of little steps go into each design. I caution you against trying to accelerate the process for the more involved projects (such as Sunflower or Dogwood) that are built through the steady accretion of many small steps. Try not to rush yourself. If you find you are growing antsy with a project, take a short break and come back to it later. Slow and steady wins the race, and the results will prove an ample reward.

TOOLS OF THE TRADE

Throughout this book I have attempted to limit the tools used to create these projects to just those items that are likely to be in the toolbox of the average crafter. You may be unfamiliar with one or two of the items featured, but all of them are easily located around the house, online, or at your neighborhood craft or office supply store. Below is a list of tools you will want to have on hand before beginning. Where applicable, I have listed a few commonly available substitutes.

Slotted Quilling Tool

This is the one tool that may be unfamiliar to you. It consists of a small metal rod with a very slender slot cut into one end. The slot is designed to grip the end of a long strip of paper in order to facilitate winding the paper into a tight coil. Such coils—sometimes referred to as scrolls, spirals, or filigree—are commonly used in the craft of quilling. I recommend purchasing a slotted quilling tool, as it will prove to be a great aid and time-saver to you.

If a slotted quilling tool is unavailable, try wrapping a strip of paper around an oversized upholstery needle. Alternatively, you can create your own quilling tool using an inexpensive bamboo skewer—the kind commonly used in cooking and available in packages at most grocery stores. Simply cut the skewer to a length you can hold comfortably in your hand—perhaps 5 inches (12.7 cm). Then, using a light touch so as not to split

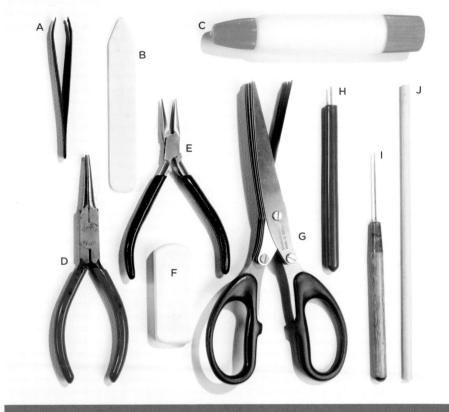

(A) TWEEZERS   (B) BONE FOLDER   (C) GLUE   (D) NEEDLE-NOSE PLIERS   (E) WIRE CUTTERS   (F) ERASER   (G) MULTI-BLADE SCISSORS   (H) QUILLING TOOL   (I) NEEDLE TOOL   (J) WOODEN DOWEL

the bamboo in two, create a small slit in one end using a craft knife. Insert a strip of paper into the cut end of the skewer, then wind the paper into a tight coil by rolling the bamboo between your thumb and forefinger. Bamboo is prone to splitting, so if you plan on making a lot of coils, purchasing an inexpensive metal quilling tool is strongly recommended.

Straightedge (aka Ruler)

A good straightedge is metal, is calibrated with $1/32$ inches or 1 mm divisions, and has a non-slip backing of cork or rubber. A long straightedge, 15 to 25 inches

(38.1 to 63.5 cm), is handy when cutting strips of paper for flower centers. A much smaller 6-inch (15.2 cm) straightedge is perfectly sized for more nimble work such as cutting Mum petals.

Hot Glue Gun

These come in a wide variety of shapes and sizes. For these projects, there is no need to spend a lot of money on a glue gun as long as the one you get has a small opening in its tip. A small opening will be very helpful in controlling the amount of glue that comes out when you squeeze the trigger.

A glue gun obviously gets hot, so in addition to not burning yourself, be sure to prevent it from burning your work surface. Many glue gun models come with a kickstand or heatproof rest. While these are useful safety features, they are not always as functional as you might expect. Kickstands often have to be folded out of the way each time you want to glue something (a maneuver requiring two hands that quickly grows tiresome), and rests are often so lightweight that they frequently tip over. Here is a tip: Consider using a small, clay flowerpot as a convenient place to rest your glue gun. Simply placing the glue gun tip-first into the pot creates a safe, stable, heatproof solution that will catch any drips and give you easy, one-handed access to your tool.

Craft Knife

Craft knives come in many shapes and sizes with blades that are fine-pointed, curved, swiveling, and oversized. For the projects included here, only the most basic craft knife is required. Find one that is not too bulky and that fits comfortably in your hand. I use a #11 Classic Fine Point blade that is angled, pointed, and has a straight metal handle. Beware of plastic handles or blade holders with cumbersome silicone grips that can interfere with the precision and control of your tool.

Stay Aware and Stay Safe

All of the tools used to create these flowers should be used with caution in order to avoid injury. Always follow the manufacturer's guidelines for proper use of such instruments. Beyond that, I have only three general safety tips to pass along to you. They are:

1. Always use sharp tools.
2. Exercise extreme caution when using those sharp tools.
3. Remember, hot glue is HOT.

The first rule is important because dull tools produce lousy results. Dull tools slip. Dull blades require more force to use, which can cause more blades to break or knives to slip. If a blade does happen to break (and they do break, with tedious frequency), stop and replace the broken blade with a fresh, unbroken one.

The second rule is perhaps one you have heard before, but if you are inexperienced using a craft knife, you may not know precisely what is entailed in the exercise of "extreme caution." Let me elaborate:

a) Use a cutting mat. Having an appropriate surface under your knife will both protect your work surface from damage and help prevent your blade from slipping as you draw it through your paper.

b) Cut carefully. Never draw a cutting blade toward your own hand or toward your own fingers.

Keep the knife firmly in your grip and always keep the fingers of your other hand safely out of harm's way when cutting. Consider using a straightedge with a non-slip backing as a guide along which to draw your knife. A non-slip straightedge will increase the accuracy of your cuts and help guard against accidental slips of your blade.

c) Wear safety glasses. If the tip of a craft knife blade breaks off, the one place you do not want that sharp little piece of metal going is into your own eye. Blades do break, so protect yourself.

The third rule—remember, hot glue is HOT—may sound obvious, but, as anyone who has used a hot glue gun can tell you, one is apt to forget this fact when one is busy concentrating on affixing two pieces of paper to one another. Hot glue oozes, and, if you get it on yourself, it is difficult to get it off quickly enough to prevent a burn. *Hot glue is never appropriate for use by children (not even with adult supervision)*, and it is only appropriate for use by adults who know enough to keep the hot tool away from both combustible surfaces and delicate skin. Always unplug your glue gun when not using it and keep it out of reach of children. In short, please be careful.

Some people hold their craft knife in their fist, as if it were a magic wand; I prefer to hold my knife between my thumb and forefingers, as if it were a pencil. This pencil-style grip ensures that my palm and wrist remain firmly on my work surface while I am cutting. This not only provides stability and control, but helps prevent my blade from slipping out from under my grip and injuring my other hand. Even if a blade breaks, my hand and wrist remain supported and stable.

Cutting Mat

Cutting mats are synthetic, non-slip surface protectors specially designed to be used with craft knives and other cutting tools. They should be placed atop your work surface (and below your paper) before cutting with a blade of any sort. They come in a wide range of sizes and are moderately priced. Cutting mats also prevent damage to your work surface that can occur when using hot glue, white adhesives, pencils, markers, and paints. They are reusable, washable, durable, and strongly recommended. If a commercially produced cutting mat is unavailable to you, a thick piece of solid cardboard or chipboard (not corrugated cardboard) will suffice. This should be thick enough and solid enough to prevent the blade of your craft knife from harming your work surface. Chipboard can be slippery when placed atop a smooth surface, so consider securing it in place using packing tape.

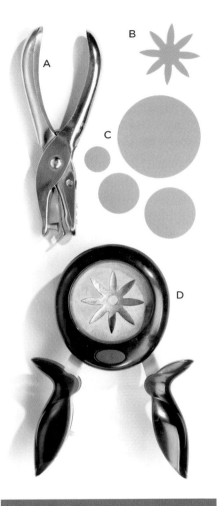

(A) ONE HOLE PUNCH
(B & C) PUNCHED PAPER
(D) DECORATIVE PAPER PUNCH

Scissors

Make sure they are sharp, as dull scissors will fray and stretch your paper. Two pairs are recommended: a standard pair of craft scissors and a small pair of sewing scissors for more detailed cutting.

Paper Punches

Nearly everything in this book can be made using little more than a pencil, scissors, and some glue. However, just because something can be accomplished using basic tools does not mean that it should only be done that way. Craft stores now offer an extensive selection of paper punches, in all shapes and sizes. Paper punches cost a little but they can greatly accelerate the process of creating certain flowers. If you decide to use a punch, be sure to buy one that has a metal cutting mechanism, a sturdy lever (a lot of force is exerted when punching through paper), and easy access to the punched-out shape (avoid punches with plastic slides that must be opened to access your punched-out paper pieces). Paper punches are tools, and as with any tool, the better the quality you can find, the more likely you are to get years of service from it.

Pliers & Wire Cutters

A small pair of needle-nose pliers is necessary for shaping floral wire into flower stems. Find a pair with a pointed tip that feels comfortable in your hand. Many needle-nose pliers also have built-in wire-cutting blades at the base of their jaws, effectively giving you two tools in one. Otherwise a separate pair of wire cutters will be needed for trimming floral wire.

Stylus

"Stylus" is simply a fancy name for a stick. Styli are useful for precisely applying glue in small amounts or in hard-to-reach places (the center of a flower blossom, for example). They can help hold things in place while glue dries (especially hot glue). They can also be used to score paper, which helps to create sharp creases. For many of these projects, a stylus is particularly useful as a form around which paper can be wrapped, coiled, and twisted.

Commercial styli made of wood, plastic, and nylon are available at craft supply stores. These tools come in a variety of sizes, from long and slender to short and stubby, and often have shaped tips that are rounded, flattened, or pointed. These tools are helpful for many craft projects, and I admit I have more than a few of them in my own toolbox.

As useful as a stylus is, you need not run out to a store to buy one. Instead, I recommend assembling a few common household items to use as substitutes. These include a #2 pencil, a medium-thick ink pen (with a straight, not tapered, barrel), a fat plastic highlighter, a pointed bamboo skewer, an old chopstick, a manicurist's cuticle stick, a pointed fingernail file, and a few small pieces of doweling (available at craft or home improvement stores in various diameters). You may not need all of these items, but a few will be useful. Begin with whatever you already have on hand and these are likely to become some of your favorite and most useful tools.

TIP: A pencil sharpener can shape more than just pencils; consider using it to add a point to a chopstick or a dowel.

Tweezers

Tiny pieces of paper, plus the occasional need for precision? You will want a pair of tweezers. Look for one with either a pointed or an angled tip.

Craft Glue

A good paper glue is one that is strong, easy to handle, and not too watery (watery glue tends to cause paper to pucker and buckle). I suggest one that is acid-free, nontoxic, washable, and a little viscous (which will prevent it from running, spreading, or dripping). You can find a wide selection of adhesives at craft and office supply stores. Rubber cement is not recommended for use with these projects.

Glue Pen

Many types of paper adhesives are available in glue pen dispensers. Such dispensers resemble plastic tubes, with one end featuring a fine-tipped applicator. Better yet, with many glue pens, once the pen is empty the tip can be removed and the plastic reservoir refilled with an adhesive of your choice. You may find a glue pen handy for these projects because it provides a convenient, no-mess way to precisely apply very small amounts of adhesive. It is not a requirement, but it is an inexpensive luxury.

DESIGN CONSIDERATIONS

Scale: How Big and How Many

The size of a blossom can make a significant difference in its visual impact. For example, a Marigold that may look adorable at 2 inches (5.1 cm) will likely look far less charming at 12 inches (30.5 cm). On the other hand, big, loopy flowers can look amazingly impressive at large scales. In general, tiny looks precious and huge looks festive, but the decision lies with you to choose what size will best work for your purposes. The projects in this book adhere mostly to the scale of real flowers.

Scale can also mean the sheer quantity of individual flowers you create. It is important to realize that you can radically alter the effects that are possible by simply increasing or decreasing the number of flowers that you create. Take, for example, the English Rose (page 38). A single English Rose has a certain whimsical quality about it that is both charming and uncomplicated, but increase the number from one to one dozen and suddenly you have a bouquet that looks luxurious, elegant, and sophisticated.

The size of your creations will suggest the type of paper you should use (and vice versa). As a general rule, thicker paper works better for larger flowers, while thinner paper works better for smaller flowers. There are limitations at both extremes, though. Extremely large flowers will be proportionally heavier,

and that may cause them to droop more than usual under their own weight. Flowers that are extremely small can be challenging to make due to their size, and working with thin and delicate paper cut into small shapes brings its own challenges. There is no foolproof equation when it comes to scale so you must rely on experimentation to guide you. Find a size that is comfortable for you, your hands, and your skills, and go from there.

Color: a Little or a Lot?

There is no denying that color will influence the overall effect of your work, so choose carefully. The decision is yours to make, but I offer the following two thoughts as guidance: 1) Often the slightly unexpected is much more pleasing to the eye than the radically unexpected, and 2) As satisfying as it can be to create a convincingly real-looking flower, there is equal pleasure to be found in letting your imagination run wild.

BOLD

For the most part, nature loves a show-off. Pale flowers can be lovely, but adding a shocking pink blossom to a bouquet of pale, pink flowers is a surefire way to enhance the whole arrangement. Flowers, stamens, foliage, and even stems come in a dizzying range of colors. A good rule of thumb is "go bold or go home." A purist may insist, for example, that

Poppies need to be red if they are to look convincingly real. The truth, though, is that Poppies come in many colors, from purple-magenta to deep red, from orange to pale yellow, and countless nuanced shades in between.

Even if you choose to stay within the expected color range for the flower you are creating, I still recommend you introduce a few minor color variations. For example, when making a vase of light-purple Asters, adding one or two Asters with a slightly darker shade of purple will make the whole bouquet look more interesting. Nature often adds a small mutation to the mix, so feel free to follow her lead.

PALE

Pale colors can be as attractive as bold colors—but be careful. Sometimes very pale colors can look a little anemic. To help guard against a washed-out look, use a lighter-than-normal green paper when creating the accompanying foliage. This will help the subtle colors of your flowers stand out and will create a sense of uniform value among all of the coordinated components (flowers, stems, and leaves).

WHITE

There are pale colors and then there is white. White flowers are especially lovely and rank as a favorite among many people. Sometimes they are associated with certain holidays, like Easter and Christmas, and certain celebrations, such as weddings and

Imperfection is Beautiful

In a book so full of step-by-step instructions, a reader might expect a word of warning regarding the importance of exactitude. Instead, I would like to offer a word of encouragement in support of imperfection. To quote a line from an old movie, "Everything beautiful is slightly lopsided." Keep in mind that not every flower need look identical to its neighbor. Do not be afraid to crinkle a petal, add a misshapen stem, or introduce a slightly different hue to a bouquet; it is their little imperfections that make flowers so endlessly fascinating and pleasurable to look at. Hand-cutting the paper shapes in the projects will add something incredible to your finished work. If you make a mistake with scissors, consider incorporating it into your design rather than starting over. A humble scrap of paper, crumpled and wadded into a ball and glued to a green stem, can, when added to an arrangement or bouquet, easily suggest a fresh, new bud or a withered, dying blossom. Far be it from me to discourage you from improving your skills, but remember that, on occasion at least, it can be quite rewarding to aspire to imperfection.

bat mitzvahs. To make the best white flowers, extra care is required when selecting paper stock and arranging the flowers into bouquets. Too many all-white blossoms in close proximity to one another can seem to disappear, with one blossom blending into another and the detail of each being lost in the overall whiteness of the group. To prevent this from happening, 1) begin with an interesting paper, and 2) be sure to include a little foliage for contrast.

If you want to use an opaque white paper, try to select one with a little "tooth"—the slightly suede-like texture found in some drawing papers. I try to avoid papers that are completely opaque, since a little light

shining through adds such an important degree of visual charm. It is equally important to understand that white can refer to a wide range of colors, from bright bluish white to pale grays and yellowy creams. My preference is to stay away from "bright white" papers in favor of natural and off-white colors. If you are creating an all-white bouquet, it is even more important that you consider using a range of whites and maybe even a sheet of beige, buff, or pale gray paper to add a little variety. This will help differentiate your flowers from one another. For an example of an all white arrangement, see page 130.

Paper: a World of Choices

It has been my experience that some ⬚ders will want to know the exact ⬚ that ar⬚ ⬚ in the ⬚. I⬚ ⬚ each ⬚ ⬚rt ⬚ ori- ⬚ ⬚ble at ⬚ also used two ⬚rticularly notewor- ⬚ors in ⬚nes ⬚n USA (reasonably ⬚nd Color-aid ⬚le in a ⬚ully ⬚c⬚ ⬚ 6- x ⬚ch (⬚ ⬚ets. ⬚wever, ⬚ ⬚aders, before spending a large sum of money on high end papers, visit the paint chip counter of their local hardware store, where a very impressive palette of colorful papers is readily available for free (in modest quantities, of course).

Before you can begin creating the flowers in this book, you must first choose an appropriate paper for the task. Countless types of paper are available at art and craft supply stores, and much of it will work very well for the projects featured in this book. However, because the available selection is so vast, a brief overview of paper stock might prove helpful in guiding you toward a selection you will be happy working with.

RECYCLED PAPER

It bears noting that paper surrounds each of us every day. It comes to us in the form of mail, magazines, and newspapers. It is found around our homes in the form of packaging, gift wrap, newsprint, coffee filters, and even labels on cans of food. Our lives are literally littered with paper. I strongly encourage you to look at the paper that already fills your world and see it as the vast, mostly untapped resource that it is. I know from experience that incredibly beautiful things are possible using only the most humble of materials.

Of the projects featured in this book, the Cattails (page 50) are made using newspaper, the Dogwood blossoms (page 93) and the Carnations (page 84) are crafted out of lowly coffee filters, and the Zinnias (page 31) are formed from paint chips. The possibilities far exceed what I have suggested. For example, the Daisies (page 54) might look just as pretty (and twice as charming) placed on a summer dinner table if made from canned corn labels. Let the materials you have on hand suggest a use.

While magazine pages can sometimes be too limp for use with some flower designs, their strength and smoothness make them an ideal medium for working out prototypes of your own designs. A page from a magazine is the perfect material for practicing a design before attempting to fabricate it with more expensive, purchased paper.

PURCHASED PAPER

Not everyone will want to rely solely on recycled papers, and for those readers, the great selection of beautiful papers available at craft stores will be a marvelous temptation. Translucent, heavy vellum and parchment papers can work very well with a few of the projects in this book, as will papers with texture or white-on-white printed patterns. Add bright colors or subtle pastels, patterns, plaids, and polka dots to the mix and the choices can seem limitless. Setting aside for a moment the considerations of paper thickness (or weight), my advice is that you find a paper that you enjoy holding in your hand, that looks pleasing when folded, and that has a color, texture, or pattern that appeals to you. Then dive into one of the tutorials.

Foliage: an Important Element

Often overlooked, foliage frames your flowers in order to show them off to their best advantage. It reinforces the "realness" of paper flowers and provides a beautiful, contrasting framework for all of your hard work. A few green leaves, or a curlicued piece of green wire, can easily add a finished look to your creation. Even more importantly, foliage adds visual interest and fullness to an arrangement and provides you an opportunity to express a great deal of personality in your creations. Think of a tall plant with gracefully arching fronds or a small violet with its textured leaves spread out beneath its flowers. If the blossom is the face of a flower, the leaves are its attire, be they bright and shiny, long and slender, or short and ragged.

When you are considering adding leaves, tendrils, and sepals (the green under-petals beneath a flower) to your arrangements, remember they need not be overly detailed to be effective. I almost always add foliage because a flower without it can sometimes look a little naked. The addition of a few leaves is all it takes to make your creation look more alive and more expressive. In the projects that follow, I have suggested a number of ways to create simple yet effective foliage. The techniques are all very easy and will help your flowers look their best.

Paper Weight Primer

Paper comes in different thicknesses, or weights. Generally speaking, thin paper is easy to handle and to cut, but if it is too thin, it may not hold its shape and may droop. Thick paper is more difficult to cut—especially small, detailed shapes—and it has more body, which can make it challenging to glue and more difficult to bend and fold into graceful shapes.

For these projects, I suggest avoiding paper weights at either extreme—tissue paper or cardstock—in favor of medium weight paper that is sturdy enough to fold, bend, and keep its shape, yet thin enough to be cut, curled, and pinched.

Sometimes paper found at art supply stores may bear a description of weight in grams. In such instances, the following summary will help you in making a selection:

80-100 gm: This is the weight of many vellum and translucent papers. It is easy to work with, folds nicely, and holds a crease. The translucent quality of these papers adds another layer of beauty to your work. Vellums, and the thinner Glassine papers, are recommended for making Poppies, Black-Eyed Susans, and Daffodils.

160 gm: This is a good, medium weight paper and is ideal for many of these flower patterns. Such papers often have a strong grain, which helps them retain their shape (especially when bent but not creased).

It can be smoothly arched into pleasing shapes, yet it is strong enough to withstand cutting into very narrow strips. Examples can be seen in the Mum and Aster patterns.

220 gm: Paper of this weight, with its added thickness and body, works perfectly for larger, heartier flowers that call for bent or curled edges. For the Tiger Lilies and Poinsettias, I have used paper of this weight in order to exploit the bendable and shapeable aspects available in papers of this thickness. Because of its firmness, 160 gm paper may require a little extra adhesive and a little more effort when rolling and shaping. But if you are comfortable working with such qualities, your results will be both sturdy and beautiful.

250-300 gm: At this weight we enter the realm of cardstock, which is not appropriate for most of the projects offered here.

The Flowers

Ranunculus To illustrate the importance of foliage, this project relies on the simplest suggestion of a flower, little more than an abstraction of a flower. Still, three facts become evident: 1) something can be beautiful without being complicated, 2) even simple skills yield attractive results, and 3) the tilt of a blossom, the bend of a wire, and the addition of a few leaves can greatly enhance any project. This project is quick and easy but it offers lessons and skills that will be applied throughout the remainder of this book.

TOOLS   SCISSORS OR CRAFT KNIFE ✳ QUILLING TOOL ✳ WHITE CRAFT GLUE ✳ HOT GLUE GUN WITH GLUE STICKS
MATERIALS   COLORFUL PAPER CUT INTO ¼- X 9-INCH (6 MM X 22.9 CM) STRIPS ✳ GREEN FLORAL WIRE (CLOTH-
COVERED IS OPTIONAL) ✳ GREEN FLORAL TAPE (OPTIONAL)

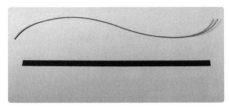

➜**1** Begin with a ¼- x 9-inch (6 mm x 22.9 cm) strip of paper and a 10- to 12-inch long (25.4 x 30.5 cm) length of floral wire.

➜**2** Using a quilling tool, wind the length of paper into a tight scroll. If you are using paper that is colored on only one side, roll the paper so that the color is on the outside of the scroll.

➜**3** Remove the coil of paper and gently loosen it with your fingers until its diameter is approximately 1 to 1 ½ inches (2.5 to 3.8 cm).

TIP: Tight coils can also be created and used to form flower buds.

➜**4** Use a tiny dot of white craft glue to secure the outer end of the scroll in place. Allow the glue to dry completely before proceeding.

➜**5** Apply a small amount of hot glue to one end of the floral wire.

➜**6** Carefully insert the wire into the center of the scroll and hold it in place until the glue is dry. Use your fingers to shape the stem so that it curves and twists in a natural manner. Add a few free-form leaves to further enhance the floral effect.

Pumpkin & Gourd
After creating a pumpkin, try your hand at a gourd. You will find that very small alterations to this basic pattern can yield dramatic results. Do not be afraid to try your own variation by changing the width of the paper strips and the manner in which you twist or turn them when threading them together.

TOOLS SCISSORS OR CRAFT KNIFE ✳ CUTTING SURFACE ✳ QUILLING NEEDLE OR SHARP EMBROIDERY NEEDLE ✳ RUBBER ERASER (OPTIONAL) ✳ NEEDLE-NOSE PLIERS ✳ WHITE CRAFT GLUE (OPTIONAL)
MATERIALS NARROW STRIPS OF PAPER IN ORANGE (ALSO IN GREEN, YELLOW, AND GRAY, FOR A GOURD) ✳ GREEN PAPER ✳ FLORAL WIRE

PUMPKIN

➜ **1** Create narrow strips of bright orange paper. I used fifteen ⅜- x 13-inch (9.5 mm x 33 cm) strips, but the number needed will vary depending on the length and width of the strips you use. Fold in half lengthwise and firmly crease each strip along its center.

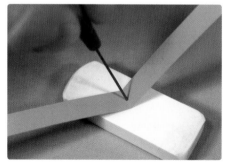

➜ **2** Use a quilling needle or a pointed embroidery needle to pierce a small hole in the center of each strip's crease. A rubber eraser makes a handy backing surface to receive the point of your needle.

➜ **3** Make sure the hole is large enough to receive a piece of green floral wire.

➜ **4** Pierce an additional hole in both ends of each folded strip.

→ **5** Use needle-nose pliers to create a small twist in one end of a 6- to 7-inch long (15.2 to 17.8 cm) piece of firm, green floral wire. Bend the twisted end 90° from the rest of the wire.

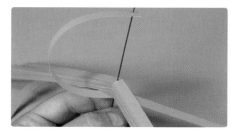

→ **6** Thread the wire through the center of each of the paper strips.

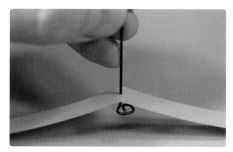

→ **7** Once all of the strips are positioned on the wire, begin looping one end of each strip onto the wire. *Note:* It is important that this step be done in a uniform manner. Loop up and thread onto the wire the bottommost strip, then repeat as you work up towards the topmost strip. Pick a direction (either left or right—just be consistent) to move around the model.

→ **8** The pumpkin at the halfway point. Continue in the same fashion, always beginning with the bottommost strip and looping it up and onto the wire, until the model is complete.

→ **9** The completed model as seen from the bottom.

→ **10** Use a pair of needle-nose pliers to create a coil in the wire at the top of the model. This creates a stem for the pumpkin and secures the strips.

→ **11** Create foliage by folding a piece of green paper in half and cutting out a basic leaf shape (template on page 122).

→ **12** Unfold the leaf and bend its tip 90°.

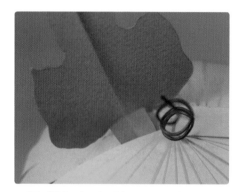

→ **13** Slide the leaf between the strips of paper. A small dot of glue can be used to prevent it from coming loose.

GOURD

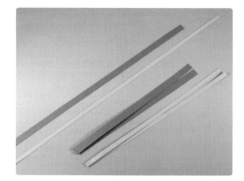

→ **1** Create strips of paper in shades of green, yellow, or gray, and feel free to vary the lengths and widths. I created 16 dark green strips, $3/8$ x 17 inches (9.5 mm x 43.2 cm), and 16 light green strips, $1/4$ x $19\,1/2$ inches (6 mm x 49.5 cm).

→ **2** As above, fold in half and crease each strip, then pierce a small hole through the center and ends of each strip. Thread all the strips onto a length of floral wire that has been prepared with a small, flat loop at one end. *Note:* Alternate between threading long and short strips, starting with one of the long strips.

→ **3** Instead of simply threading one strip after another as with the pumpkin, treat each *pair* of strips— one long and one short—as a single group. Beginning with the bottom-most *pair* of strips, thread the shorter strip onto the wire.

→ **5** Once the first *pair* of strips is looped into place, continue with the next *pair* of strips. Always loop the longer strip (twisted once) onto the wire after the shorter strip.

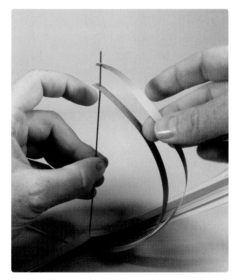

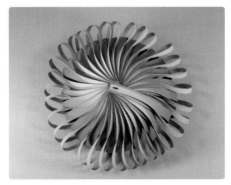

→ **4** After the shorter strip is in place, twist the second, longer strip once before threading it onto the wire.

→ **6** When all of the strips have been threaded onto the wire, use pliers to bend a small, tight loop in the end that protrudes from the top of the gourd.

→ **7** The finished gourd as seen from above. Gently straighten and arrange all of the strips until they are distributed uniformly around the model.

Aster Asters have long been known as a symbol of patience. I'll admit that for some flowers, meticulously cutting and shaping individual petals is necessary to get a pleasing result. However, office supply and craft stores are filled with clever and useful tools and, whenever I find one that can save me time while helping me create something lovely, I wholeheartedly endorse taking the easy way out.

TOOLS STRAIGHTEDGE * PENCIL OR PEN * SCISSORS (OR MULTI-BLADE SHREDDING SCISSORS) * HOT GLUE GUN AND GLUE STICKS * WHITE GLUE * 1½-INCH (3.8 CM) 8-POINT STAR PAPER PUNCH * 1½-INCH (3.8 CM) SCALLOPED PAPER PUNCH **MATERIALS** PURPLE, YELLOW, AND GREEN PAPER * A BOTTLE CORK * FLORAL WIRE

➜**1** Begin with three strips of 2- x 16-inch (5.1 x 40.6 cm) paper. Using a straightedge and a pencil, draw a line ¼ inch (6 mm) below the top edge along the length of the first strip. On the second strip, mark a line that is ½ inch (1.3 cm) below the top edge. On the third strip, draw a line that is 1 inch (2.5 cm) below the top edge. Use standard scissors, or for greater speed, multi-blade shredding scissors (shown on page 9) to cut slits from the bottom edge of each strip to each penciled line. Cut these slits along the entire length of each strip.

➜**2** Wind around a cork the strip with the shortest fringe. For this first layer only, be sure to align the top of the cork with the bottom of the fringe. A dot of hot glue at the beginning will help secure the strip as it is wound, and another at the end will secure the strip after it is wound.

➜**3** Wrap the strip with medium fringe over the first strip and secure it with hot glue. Be sure to align the top of the fringe on this second layer with the top of the fringe on the first layer.

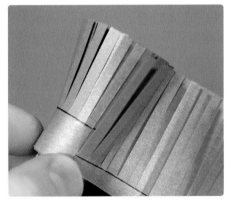

➜**4** Add the third layer of paper by wrapping the strip with the longest fringe around the first two strips. Secure the paper with glue. Be sure to align the top of the fringe on this third layer with the tops of the fringe on the previous two layers.

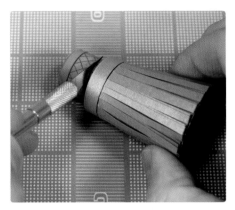

➜**5** You may wish to carefully trim with a craft knife whatever portion of the cork protrudes from the bottom of the flower.

➜**6** A few petals at a time, unfold and open the entire blossom.

TIP: It may help to apply slight pressure to the bases of the petals in order to prevent them from folding closed again.

→ **7** When all of the petals have been shaped, the aster should look like this.

→ **8** For the center of the flower you will need three 8-point stars. If a punch is not available, the flower centers can be hand cut using scissors.

TIP: Precision is not required since a little variation will only enhance the flower's look.

→ **9** Use a small dot of white glue to affix the centers of two stars.

→ **10** Add a third star and, to add height, bend the petals upwards.

→ **11** Use another dot of hot glue to affix the flower center to the top of the cork. Hold in place until the glue has dried. Turn the flower over and affix a wire stem to the base of the cork with hot glue.

→ **12** To create the leaves of the foliage, I used a 1½-inch (3.8 cm) scalloped hole punch and a common ¼-inch (6 mm) punch to add an offset hole near the edge of each leaf. To

attach each leaf, simply slide the stem into the small hole, position the leaf somewhere along the stem, fold the edges upwards, and glue in place. Use the photograph on page 28 as a guide for placement of the leaves.

Zinnia I once lived next to a modest gardener, a hobbyist who was happy with a few simple marigolds and petunias in her flower beds. However, she always made sure to plant a few rows of Zinnias along the sunny side of her house. That side of her house was not visible through any window nor could one view it from the yard. Nevertheless, she planted there. "Butterflies love zinnias," she used to say, "and every garden is judged not only by the flowers in it, but also by those creatures it attracts." I include a few zinnias here because what is true of gardens is also true of life.

TOOLS PENCIL ✳ STRAIGHTEDGE ✳ CRAFT KNIFE ✳ SLOTTED QUILLING TOOL ✳ HOT GLUE GUN AND GLUE STICKS ✳ SCISSORS **MATERIALS** PAINT CHIPS (OR BRIGHTLY COLORED PAPER) ✳ GREEN PAPER ✳ FLORAL WIRE ✳ GREEN FLORAL TAPE

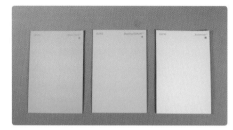

➜ **1** Select a few coordinated paint chips (available from hardware and home improvement stores). The paint chips used in this example are 3½ x 5 inches (8.9 x 12.7 cm). You can use any vaguely rectangular chip regardless of whether it is larger or smaller than this.

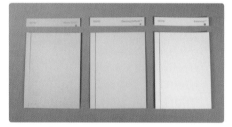

➜ **2** Trim off any identifying text or insignia. Use a straightedge and pencil to draw a line the length of your rectangle and approximately ¼ inch (6 mm) in from edge.

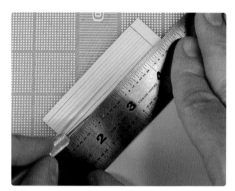

➜ **3** Using a straightedge as a guide, cut narrow strips until you have fringed the entire rectangle. Be sure to NOT cut into the ¼-inch (6 mm) strip.

➜ **4** Repeat the process of cutting fringe into two other pieces. You can use more than three colors if you wish.

➜ **5** Insert the ¼-inch (6 mm) edge of your paper into the slotted quilling tool and roll the paper into a tight coil. Secure the end with hot glue—craft glue is often not strong enough for use with paint chips. Roll and then glue the next piece of fringed paper on top of the first. Perform the same step with the last fringed piece.

➜ **6** When all three pieces of paper have been wound into a tight coil and glued in place, remove the quilling tool. Add a small amount of hot glue to the bottom of the coil to further secure the paper in place.

→ 7 Hold the coil with one hand and with the other, unfold and shape the petals.

→ 8 The finished blossom will have subtle variations of color intermixed among its petals. Affix a length of floral wire, wrapped with green floral tape, to the back of the flower.

→ 9 To create foliage, cut out a leaf shape from a piece of folded green paper, or use the template on page 123. Use scissors to create cuts angled down toward the stem of the leaf.

→ 10 Unfold the leaf and shape it by curving the petal downward, exposing the cuts made in step 9.

→ 11 Leaves can be attached to the stem of the flower by using a short length of tightly wrapped green floral tape.

→ 12 The yellow flower was made using solid color paint chips. The red flower was made using multiple-color paint chips.

Mum The glories of spring and summer flowers are well known. However, in the Northeast, when the leaves begin to fall and the weather turns cool, I always look forward to the arrival of mums. They come in a wide variety of shapes and sizes but my favorite type are the hardy, decorative blossoms with pompom-shaped flowers and delicately curved petals. Best of all, mums come in a dizzying range of colors, from pastels to vibrant yellows to rich autumn hues. This project shows you how to turn almost any small sheet of colorful paper into an exuberant and graceful flower.

TOOLS PENCIL * STRAIGHTEDGE * CRAFT KNIFE * QUILLING TOOL * HOT GLUE GUN AND GLUE STICKS
MATERIALS COLORED PAPER (THIN AND STRONG) * GREEN PAPER FOR FOLIAGE * WHITE CRAFT GLUE
* TWINE-COVERED FLORAL WIRE * GREEN FLORAL TAPE

→**1** The 3½- x 5- inch (8.9 x 12.7 cm) sheet of pale green paper used in this example will yield a flower that is approximately 4 inches (10.2 cm) in diameter. Feel free to use a larger or smaller piece depending on the desired size of your flnished flower.

→**2** On the back of the rectangle, use a pencil to draw a line ¼ inch (6 mm) in from each of the two short sides.

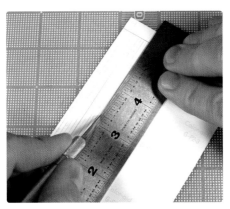

→**3** Using a straightedge as a guide along which to draw your craft knife, cut narrow strips along the length of the rectangle. Cut only between the two lines drawn in step 2.

TIP: Be sure to hold the guide firmly in place so that it does not slip. Take your time and cut each strip carefully and evenly.

→**4** The narrower the strips, the more frilly and delicate the final flower will look—the wider the strips, the bolder and hardier. In the example, each strip is just under ⅛ inch (3 mm) wide.

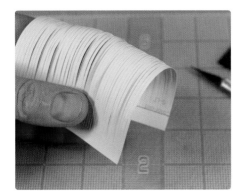

→**5** Place an index finger behind the paper and coax the cut strips into a gently curved shape. Be careful not to crease the strips since you want a very elegant loop-shape for this flower.

TIP: To help shape the strips you can partially wrap the cut paper over the shaft of a wide highlighter pen or the handle of a wooden spoon.

→**6** After pre-bending the paper, apply a small dot of white glue to one of the back corners. Do not glue along the entire edge because the flower will not form properly.

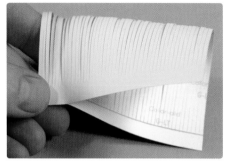

→ 7 Gently bring the top corner down to the bottom corner and hold it in place until the glue has dried completely. Remember to glue only the one corner, not the entire edge.

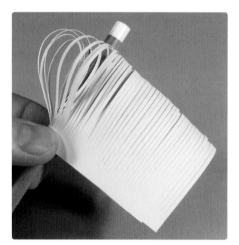

→ 8 Beginning with the glued corner, carefully wind the paper snugly around the shaft of a pencil or small dowel. Notice in the photo that the pencil extends above the loops; this will help prevent the loops from becoming tangled. As you wind the paper around the pencil, be sure to keep the unglued edges aligned.

→ 9 Once you have completed wrapping the paper around the pencil, glue down the ends and firmly hold them in place until the glue has dried completely. If you let go before the glue has dried, your flower will unravel and your loops may become bent and misshapen.

→ 10 Carefully insert a finger into the very center of the petals and gently bend them outward to open up and shape your flower.

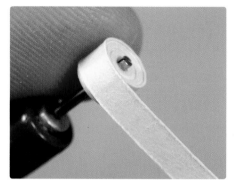

→ 11 Use a quilling tool to scroll a narrow strip of paper into a spiral.

→ 12 Insert the scrolled paper strip into the bottom of the flower, allowing it to unravel a little so that it fits snugly into the hole left by the pencil or dowel used in step 8.

→ 13 Add a generous dot of white craft glue to the paper scroll and allow it to dry completely. Use a daub of hot glue to add a wire stem to the flower.

→ 14 To finish your blossom, simply wrap the wire stem with green floral tape, and include a few free-form leaves if desired.

English Rose   The design for this English rose was shown to me by a seamstress who had herself learned it from a quilter. I suspect I am not the first person to translate the design into paper, but that does not detract from its beauty. This little blossom has a great deal of charm when made from beautifully patterned papers. Create the same design using white and off-white paper for a result that is instantly more formal and elegant. Ambitious crafters may consider watercoloring paper before cutting out the spiral shape. The results will be spectacular.

TOOLS SCISSORS OR CRAFT KNIFE ✳ BAMBOO SKEWER (OR SMALL DOWEL) ✳ HOT GLUE GUN AND GLUE STICKS ✳ SMALL NEEDLE-NOSE PLIERS **MATERIALS** PAPER* ✳ FLORAL WIRE ✳ GREEN FLORAL TAPE (OPTIONAL)

Origami papers are the perfect thickness and are available in many beautiful patterns. Scrapbook papers are also appropriate (though avoid cardstock weights) and come in a wide variety of designs and colors.

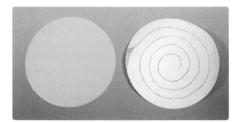

→**1** Begin with a circle of paper that is thin enough to be easily curled. Your circle can be of any size, and in fact I encourage you to utilize multiple, differently sized circles to create variation and interest in a bouquet. For this example, a circle of roughly 7 inches (17.8 cm) works nicely as a starting point. Cut the disk into a spiral as indicated on the template on page 125.

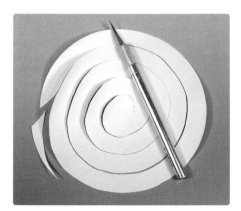

→**2** When creating the spiral, a small, irregular shape will be formed where the beginning spiral meets the second spiral ring. Remove and discard this small, elongated triangle of paper, as shown.

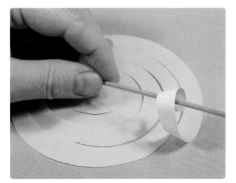

→**3** Starting with the outermost end of the spiral, begin winding the paper around a bamboo skewer or a thin piece of dowel.

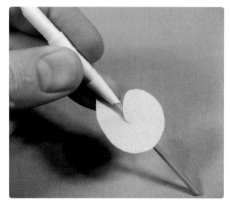

→**4** Wind the paper snugly around the bamboo skewer until you get to the center of the paper disk. Because of the uneven shape of the paper, it will naturally extend a bit down the length of the skewer as you wind it.

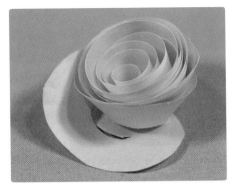

place, making sure the bottom edges of the coiled paper make contact with the adhesive. Hold in place until the glue has dried.

➡ **5** Remove the skewer. The paper should unravel slightly, leaving you with a loosely spooled coil. If your paper does not unravel as much as you would like, gently unwind it by hand, then loosely rewind it by hand to get your desired size and shape.

➡ **6** Hold the spiraled portion of the paper out of the way and apply a large dot of hot glue to the unspiraled center. Then position the spiraled paper over the glue and press it into

➡ **7** Dried glue should be clear and not overly visible in the finished flower.

→ **8** Use small needle-nose pliers to create a tiny loop in the end of a piece of floral wire. I used thread-covered floral wire, but regular wire wrapped with green floral tape can be used instead. Attach the stem to the flower with a small dot of hot glue. Hold everything in place until the glue dries.

Wild Violet   Not every flower needs to be arranged in an elaborate bouquet or vase. Sometimes, what is called for is a tiny bloom, just large enough to catch someone's eye or punctuate a place setting at a dinner table. These charmers take but a few minutes to make using only a few pieces of paper and a pin. This is one example where less is definitely more.

TOOLS 1½-INCH (3.8 CM) STAR OR FLOWER-SHAPED PAPER PUNCH ✳ WHITE CRAFT GLUE ✳ ERASER ✳ SCISSORS ✳ HOT GLUE GUN AND GLUE STICKS (OPTIONAL) **MATERIALS** COLORFUL PAPER (INCLUDING GREEN) ✳ PEARL-HEAD PINS (VARIOUS COLORS) ✳ 26-GAUGE WIRE ✳ GREEN FLORAL TAPE ✳ A QUARTER OR SMALL METAL WASHER (OPTIONAL)

➔ **1** Use the paper punch to create four shapes. Three of these shapes will form the petals of the flower and should be made using colorful paper, while the fourth will form the sepals (under-petals) and should be made using green paper.

➔ **2** Stack all four paper shapes atop one another (with the green piece on the bottom) and pierce the center of the stack using a pearl-head pin.

TIP: Try using an eraser under the flower shapes to receive the sharp point of the pin.

➔ **3** Once you have created a pin-hole in the center of each shape, fold the petals of the top shapes upward (left), stack two other shapes with their petals off-set (center) and affix using craft glue, and fold the petals of the green shape downward (right).

➔ **4** Slide the pieces in the order shown, onto the pearl-headed pin, adding a dot of white craft glue between each layer.

TIP: Place the pin in the eraser while the glue dries.

➔ **5** Twist a length of pliable, 26-gauge wire around the stem of the pin. Affix pin to stem with a dot of craft glue. Allow to dry completely.

➔ **6** Wrap the wire with a piece of green floral tape.

➜ **7** To create the foliage for this flower, accordion-pleat a piece of green paper approximately 4 x 6 inches (10.2 x 15.2 cm), as shown. I have used five pleats, but you may add as many or as few as you desire.

➜ **10** Holding the pleated paper as shown (with the crease at the top and open edges at the bottom), gently pull the pleats along the top apart to create a slight curved shape.

➜ **11** The finished leaf will have the segmented appearance of a lobster's tail.

➜ **8** Fold the pleated paper in half.

➜ **9** Trim the pleated paper into a semi-circle.

→ 12 To make the flower stand up, make a small hole in the base of the leaf or leaves, and thread the stem through. Hot glue the wire stem to a quarter or small metal washer to create a weighted base.

Allium   Alliums, those wonderfully whimsical ball-shaped flowers, are actually each made up of hundreds of tiny flowers clustered together on an array of radiating stems. Recreating such blossoms might seem challenging at first, but with the help of a single, decorative paper punch, the process is quite simple and the results are beautiful.

TOOLS 1½-INCH (3.8 CM) STAR- OR FLOWER-SHAPED PAPER PUNCH * HOT GLUE GUN AND GLUE STICKS
MATERIALS PAPER IN A VARIETY OF ANALOGOUS COLORS (REDS OR PURPLES) * 1½-INCH (3.8 CM) DIAMETER
POLYSTYRENE FOAM BALLS * BRIGHT GREEN PAPER * GREEN, TWINE-WRAPPED FLORAL WIRE * FLORAL
FROG (OPTIONAL)

➜ **1** Begin with a selection of colorful paper; I favor reds and purples but any hues will work. Select a star- or flower-shaped paper punch and cut out shapes. I have used a 1½-inch (3.8 cm) diameter 8-point star for this example.

➜ **2** Work your way around the piece, folding the petals of each shape in toward the center.

➜ **3** Create enough shapes to cover a small polystyrene foam ball. For this example I punched out and folded 22 star shapes in order to cover a 1½-inch diameter (3.8 cm) ball.

→ **4** Use a dot of hot glue to affix the folded pieces of paper one by one to the polystyrene foam ball. Begin by attaching eight pieces around the circumference of the ball and then add one to the top center and bottom center of each ball. Fill in the remaining area with six additional pieces. ***Note:*** Hot glue can melt polystyrene foam, so it is best to apply the glue to the back of each paper piece instead of to the ball itself.

→ **5** Once all of the pieces have been attached and the glue has dried completely, carefully unfold each paper star to create the blossom.

TIP: A small pointed tool, such as a manicure stick, plastic stylus, or a crochet hook, may be helpful when unfolding the paper.

→ **6** Allium foliage usually grows low to the ground and is somewhat tangled-looking. To create this effect, begin with a strip of green paper 20 inches (50.8 cm) long by ¾ inch (1.9 cm) wide. Fold the paper in half lengthwise, as shown at far left in the photo. Then fold the paper again widthwise (center). Pull the two layers apart slightly and round the tips with a pair of scissors (far right). Gently shape the leaves by curling the flattened shapes with a finger as you might curl a piece of ribbon.

→ **7** Add a stem by inserting a length of twine-covered floral wire into the polystyrene foam ball and securing it with hot glue. Foliage can be added by loosely inserting it into the holes of a floral frog, or by attaching it to the base of each stem with hot glue.

Cattail   The distinction between a "flower" and a "weed" can be a slim one, and often it is one that exists in name only (think of wild daisies). In the broadest sense of the word, a flower is an attractive ornament that provides a horticultural snapshot of the season. Cattails fit this bill perfectly: New growth begins in early spring, mature flowers are visible all summer long, rich brown blossoms fade to white and gray in the autumn, and brown stalks stand guard in the landscape all winter long.

TOOLS 1¼-INCH (3.2 CM) PAPER PUNCH (SCALLOP-EDGED OR CIRCULAR) ✳ ¼-INCH (6 MM) HOLE PUNCH ✳ SCISSORS OR CRAFT KNIFE ✳ HOT GLUE GUN AND GLUE STICKS **MATERIALS** BROWN, OPAQUE PAPER (OR NEWSPRINT) ✳ HEAVY-DUTY FLORAL WIRE (OR VERY THIN WOOD DOWELING) ✳ BROWN OR DARK GREEN FLORAL TAPE ✳ CLEAR PLASTIC STRAWS ✳ GREEN PAPER

➜**1** Using a paper punch, cut out thirty 1¼-inch diameter (3.2 cm) circular shapes from the brown paper. Use a ¼-inch (6 mm) common hole punch to make a small opening in the center of each disk.

➜**3** Use scissors to trim a clear plastic drinking straw into ⅛- to ¼-inch (3 to 6 mm) pieces. ***Note:*** Be sure that the diameter of the drinking straw is larger than the diameter of the hole in the center of each disk.

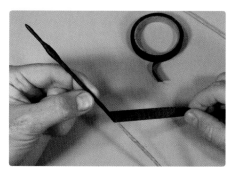

➜**2** Wrap a length of ⅛-inch-wide (3 mm) paper-wrapped floral wire with brown or dark green floral tape. You may substitute a length of very thin wooden doweling if you prefer. Use an additional length of floral tape to create a slight bulge near the tip of the stem (see photo). This bulge should be thick enough to prevent the disks of paper from slipping off the ends of their stems.

➜**4** Working from the bottom of the stem (opposite the bulge), alternate between adding disks of paper and clear plastic straw spacers.

→ **5** Once you have added enough disks and spacers to create a cattail of the desired size (I used 30 disks for this example), prevent the disks from slipping off the stem by creating another bulge of floral tape below the bottommost disk.

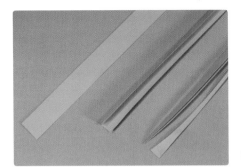

→ **6** Cattail foliage can be made with a strip of green, yellow, or brown paper approximately 1 inch (2.5 cm) wide and 10 to 18 inches (25.4 to 45.7 cm) long. Fold the strip in half along its length. Using scissors or a craft knife, trim the top few inches into a spear shape. Attach the leaves at the base using hot glue.

TIP: Consider grouping your cattails together in thickets of three, five, or seven. For variations in the color and texture of your cattails, you can use brown craft paper, plain newsprint, or recycled newspapers as your paper stock. Old and yellowed paper will give your design the suggestion of a cattail gone to seed.

→ **7** Fashion a stand from wire and hot glue it to the base of the cattail.

Daisy   One of the secrets to creating beautiful paper flowers is to keep things simple. The suggestion of detail is often enough to create the illusion. This is especially useful when creating flowers for large-scale celebrations such as weddings. When hundreds of flowers need to be made, this is exactly the sort of design you will want to use. Much of the work is accomplished with a paper punch. A few steps, such as cutting the petals with scissors and bending the petals into shape, can be accomplished while watching TV or engaging in some other activity. The job will go even faster if you include a few friends in the process.

TOOLS 3-INCH (7.6 CM) PAPER PUNCH (OR SCISSORS) ✳ SCISSORS OR CRAFT KNIFE ✳ HOT GLUE GUN AND GLUE STICKS **MATERIALS** WHITE PAPER ✳ YELLOW PAPER ✳ FLORAL WIRE ✳ GREEN FLORAL TAPE

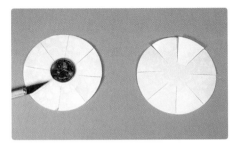

➜**1** Begin with a 3-inch (7.6 cm) disk of paper—a circular paper-punch is a great help here. Using a craft knife, make eight evenly spaced incisions, leaving an uncut section in the center of the disk that is about the size of a quarter. These cuts can be made freehand with scissors since absolute precision is not necessary.

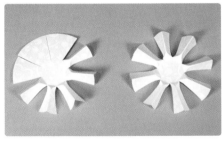

➜**2** Fold the tip of each petal in half using your thumb and forefinger. Gently continue the crease of each petal as close as possible to the center of each disk.

➜**3** Glue together two fully creased disks, making sure that the petals of the bottom disk align between the petals of the top disk.

➜**4** Tightly wind a ⅛- x 13-inch (3 mm x 33 cm) piece of yellow paper into a scroll and affix it to the center of the daisy.

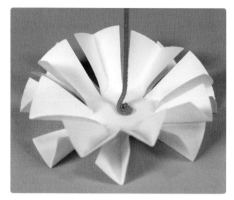

→ **5** To ensure that your daisy remains securely attached to its stem, add a small twist to the tip of each wire before affixing it to the back of the blossom using a generous amount of hot glue. Finish the stem by wrapping it with green floral tape.

Dahlia Once you have mastered making daisies (page 54), it is time to move on to dahlias. Like that flower, this blossom is composed of simple circles and a few carefully placed cuts. Creating the density of these flowers requires a little more time; however, the results are so lovely and lush that they are worth the extra effort and patience required. Dahlias come in almost every color, so choose the hues you favor most.

TOOLS PAPER PUNCHES IN A RANGE OF SIZES* ✳ PENCIL ✳ STRAIGHTEDGE ✳ SCISSORS OR CRAFT KNIFE ✳ HOT GLUE GUN AND GLUE STICKS **MATERIALS** BRIGHTLY COLORED PAPER IN SHADES OF A SINGLE COLOR ✳ A QUARTER AND A NICKEL ✳ GREEN PAPER FOR FOLIAGE ✳ HEAVY GAUGE FLORAL WIRE ✳ GREEN FLORAL TAPE

3-, 2-, and 1-inch-diameter (7.6, 5.1, and 2.5 cm) punches are recommended.

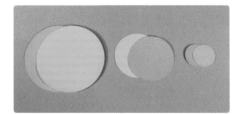

➜**1** Create with paper punches two 3-inch (7.6 cm), two 2-inch (5.1 cm), and two 1-inch (2.5 cm) circles, or cut them out using scissors. **_Note:_** For this design it is recommended that you use six analogous colors (colors that are next to one another on a color wheel.) These could be six colors in the yellow family, six colors in the purple family, etc. You can also use three similar colors (or even two similar colors) as long as you only repeat colors on differently sized disks (no two disks of the same size should be the same color).

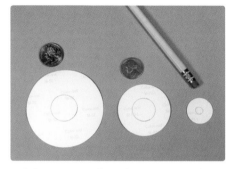

➜**2** Draw a small circle on the back of each disk, as shown.

TIP: I used a quarter, a nickel, and the end of a pencil eraser on the 3-, 2- and 1-inch (7.6, 5.1, and 2.5 cm) disks respectively.

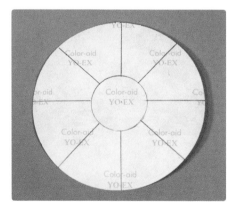

➜**3** Using a straight edge and a pencil, divide each disk into eight equal segments. Cut along each line using a craft knife or scissors. **_Note:_** Do not cut into the center circle.

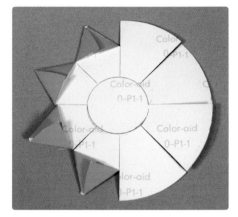

➜**4** Fold the edges of each segment inward to form a point.

➜**5** To add dimension to the petals, turn the disk over and firmly pinch each pointed tip. Repeat steps 3 through 5 for the five remaining disks.

→ **6** Stack like-sized pieces atop one another in pairs, as shown, so that their pointed tips are offset. Connect each pair using a dot of hot glue. Allow the glue to dry.

→ **7** Attach the three pairs of disks using hot glue. Press the pieces together using the end of a pencil until the glue is dry.

→ **8** Create the sepals (under-petals) with a 3-inch (7.6 cm) disk of green paper, folded as in step 4. However, rather than pinching the pointed tips, crease the paper between the points, as shown.

→ **9** Position the sepals and flower, as shown. ***Note:*** The green paper should be positioned smooth-side up; the flower should be positioned with its underside facing up. Add a small dot of hot glue to the center of the flower portion.

→ **10** Carefully attach the sepals to the back of your flower, as shown.

→ **11** For a stem, attach a thick, floral-tape-wrapped wire using hot glue.

TIP: Raffia-covered floral wire is thicker than regular floral wire and works well for these stems. You can also use a wire hanger. To do so, remove with a wire-cutter a length of wire from the hanger, straighten the wire with your hands, and then wrap it with green floral tape before attaching it to your flower. (*Note:* It is easiest to wrap these thick wires with floral tape before attaching them to the stem.)

→ **12** If you wish to add foliage, cut out leaves using the template on page 122 and affix to the stem using green floral tape.

White Flower As nice as it can be to create a flower based on a real cultivar, conjuring up a design from your own imagination can be just as satisfying. While this little blossom has no real-world antecedent, that has not stopped it from becoming one of my most popular designs. These white flowers look especially nice when many individual blossoms are grouped together. There is no foliage, so be sure to pay special attention to making the long, wire stems as graceful and expressive as possible.

TOOLS 3-INCH (7.6 CM) PAPER PUNCH ✳ SCISSORS OR CRAFT KNIFE ✳ NEEDLE-NOSE PLIERS
MATERIALS WHITE PAPER* ✳ WHITE GLUE ✳ 22-GAUGE GREEN FLORAL WIRE ✳ GREEN FLORAL TAPE

*Vellum, white-on-white, or colorful patterned papers work equally well. Whatever type you choose,
be sure it is lightweight if you wish to recreate the look of the delicate blossoms illustrated in the example.*

➔**1** Cut a 3-inch (7.6 cm) disk of
paper (a hole punch is helpful, though
scissors will also work). Fold the disk
in half, then again into quarters, and
then once more into eighths.

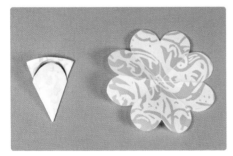

➔**2** Use scissors to round the wide
end of the segment, as shown. Unfold
the paper to reveal an 8-petal disk.

➔**3** Use scissors to remove one of
the petals.

➔**4** Close the gap created in step
3 by overlapping the two petals and
affixing them with a dot of white craft
glue. Hold in place until dry.

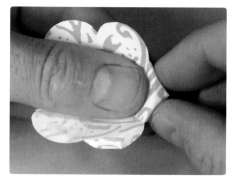

→ **5** Put the finishing touch on the blossom by gently crimping the end of each petal between your thumb and forefinger.

→ **6** The finished blossom is simple and elegant.

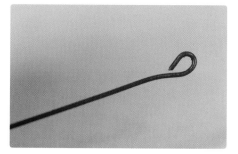

→ **7** Use needle-nose pliers to create a small loop in one end of a 15-inch (38.1 cm) length of floral wire.

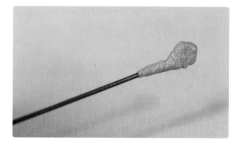

→ **8** Cover the loop with a 1-inch (2.5 cm) length of green floral tape.

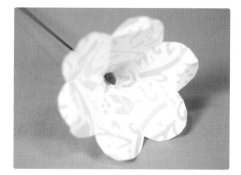

→ **9** Carefully thread the wire through the center of the flower (the tip of the wire should easily puncture the paper). Gently pull the stem down until the loop is firmly positioned in the center of the flower.

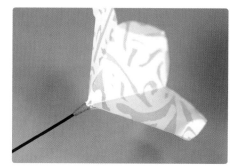

→ **10** Gently pull the stem into the flower until a small portion of floral tape protrudes from the base.

TIP: If the paper tears a little, a small amount of hot glue can be used to stabalize the stem before proceeding.

→ **11** Beginning at the base of the paper flower, wrap the entire stem with a length of green floral tape, making sure the tape is wrapped tightly around the paper flower to hold it in place. These flowers look best atop stems that are gracefully arched and curled.

Black-Eyed Susan   The simple shape and winning charm of Black-Eyed Susans make them a favorite of gardeners everywhere, and these Black-Eyed Susans can be made using only simple tools, a few pieces of wire, and a sheet of cheery, translucent paper. The challenge of creating a "climbing" vine is solved by letting the flowers hang off a central support rather than rest atop bulky stems.

TOOLS 2-INCH (5.1 CM) PAPER PUNCH ✳ SCISSORS OR CRAFT KNIFE ✳ WHITE CRAFT GLUE ✳ QUILLING TOOL ✳ TWEEZERS (OPTIONAL) ✳ NEEDLE-NOSE PLIERS ✳ HOT GLUE GUN AND GLUE STICKS **MATERIALS** ORANGE TRANSLUCENT PAPER ✳ STRIPS OF BLACK PAPER ⅛ X 6-INCHES (3 MM X 15.2 CM) ✳ FLORAL WIRE ✳ GREEN FLORAL TAPE

Medium-weight vellum paper works well

➜ 1 Precision is important when creating this design, so use a paper punch to cut 2-inch (5.1 cm) disks of translucent orange paper.

➜ 2 Fold the disk of paper in half to create a semi-circle shape.

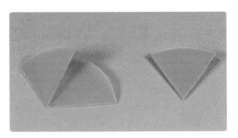

➜ 3 Fold the semi-circle into thirds.

➜ 4 Use scissors or a craft knife to trim the upper edge of the pie shape, as shown.

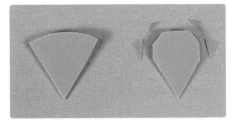

➜ 5 Unfold the modified pie-shaped piece of paper. The model should now resemble a six-petal flower.

➜ 6 Using scissors or a craft knife, make a small incision between two of the petals of the flower.

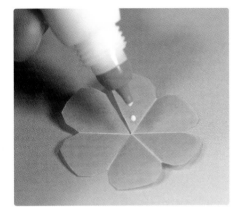

➜ 7 Apply a very small amount of glue to one of the petals near the incision.

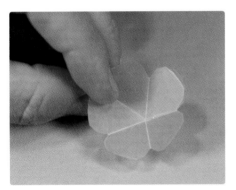

➜ 8 Glue the petals on each side of the incision to one another by stacking one on top of the other and holding the pieces in place until the glue dries completely. You should now have a five-petal flower.

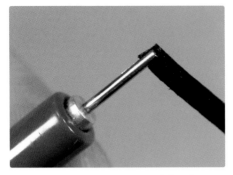

→ **9** To create the center of the flower, use a quilling tool and a ⅛- x 6-inch (3 mm x 12.7 cm) strip of black paper.

→ **10** Wind the strip of paper into a tight scroll.

→ **11** Secure the end of the scroll with a tiny dot of glue and hold in place until dry.

→ **12** To attach the center to the blossom, place a medium dot of glue in the center of each flower.

→ **13** Using your fingers or a pair of tweezers, place the black scroll in the center of the flower and allow the glue to dry completely.

→ **14** Repeat steps 2 through 13 for additional flowers.

→ **15** Using needle-nose pliers, bend a length of floral wire into an "S"-shaped scroll (I used thread-covered floral wire).

→ **16** These scrolls will serve as foliage for the flower, so create them in a variety of shapes and sizes.

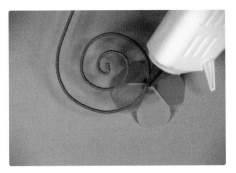

→ **17** Affix flowers to foliage using dabs of hot glue. Allow glue to cool completely before handling.

→ **18** To display the finished flowers, affix a tall, straight piece of wire to a weighted base, bend the top of the wire into a small hook, and hang the foliage pieces from the hook, interlocking them with one another to create a vine as long or as short as you desire.

Cosmos

Cosmos have a lovely, yet slightly unruly quality often found in wildflowers. Nothing could be simpler or more sophisticated at the same time. Translucent or vellum-type papers are particularly well suited for this project and will enhance the delicate look of the flower petals by allowing a little light to shine through. Cosmos come in many colors—from yellows and oranges to pinks, reds, and whites—so choose any color you like best.

TOOLS 2-INCH (5.1 CM) ROUND PAPER PUNCH ✳ SCISSORS OR CRAFT KNIFE ✳ WHITE CRAFT GLUE ✳ HOT GLUE GUN AND GLUE STICKS **MATERIALS** PINK TRANSLUCENT PAPER ✳ STRIPS OF YELLOW PAPER, 1/8 X 6 INCHES (3 MM X 15.2 CM) ✳ GREEN TRANSLUCENT PAPER ✳ GREEN FLORAL WIRE

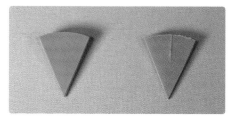

➜ **1** Use a hole punch to create a 2-inch (5.1 cm) disk of paper. Fold the disk in half, then into quarters, and finally into eighths. Use scissors or a craft knife to make a 1/4- to 1/2-inch (6 mm to 1.3 cm) incision in the folded disk, as shown.

➜ **2** Unfold the paper and gently press the creases flat with your finger.

➜ **3** Fold the edges of each incision in toward each seam to create eight pointed petals.

➜ **4** Turn the flower over so that the folds face down.

➜ **5** Using scissors or a craft knife, cut off the pointed tip of each petal.

➜ **6** Roll a 1/8 x 6-inch (3 mm x 15.2 cm) strip of yellow paper into a loose scroll. Secure the end of the scroll to keep it from further unraveling, then affix it with a dot of craft glue to the center of the flower.

69

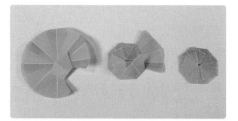

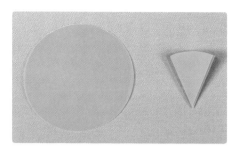

→ **7** To make the flowers look more natural, you can add flower buds to the arrangement of fully opened flowers. To do so, begin with the same incised disks from step 1 and fold each petal inwards to the center of the disk, working your way around in one direction. Tuck the edge of the final petal behind the edge of the first petal to complete.

→ **9** To complete the overall design, add small, green sepals (under-petals) beneath the flowers. Make these by folding 2-inch (5.1 cm) disks of green paper into eighths, as in step 1.

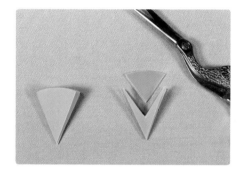

→ **10** Using scissors or a craft knife, cut a pie-shaped notch out of each folded disk, as shown.

→ **8** To give your flower bud a slightly cupped shape, fold the entire bud in half in one direction, then unfold and make a similar fold perpendicular to the first.

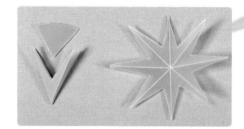

→ **11** Gently unfold the remainder of each disk to reveal star-shaped sepals.

→ **12** Affix each flower blossom to a sepal. Attach wire stems using hot glue and then gently shape your flowers into a pleasing arrangement.

Orchid The orchid presents a curious and challenging case for the paper crafter. By itself, each of its elements barely suggests anything botanical, let alone anything beautiful. But combine the elements—the interwoven disks of bright paper, the slender stem, the broad, thick leaves—and the result is instantly recognizable as an orchid. The simplicity of the structure itself translates into elegance, but be careful when applying glue, because there is nowhere to hide a mistake in this spare design.

TOOLS 3-INCH (7.6 CM) PAPER PUNCH ✳ PENCIL ✳ SCISSORS OR CRAFT KNIFE ✳ WHITE CRAFT GLUE ✳ HOT GLUE GUN AND GLUE STICKS ✳ ¼-INCH (6 MM) PAPER PUNCH **MATERIALS** FUCHSIA TRANSLUCENT PAPER FOR FLOWERS* ✳ GREEN FLORAL WIRE ✳ GREEN FLORAL TAPE ✳ GREEN OPAQUE PAPER FOR FOLIAGE

I recommend brightly colored paper that is translucent. If such paper is unavailable, opaque paper will also work.

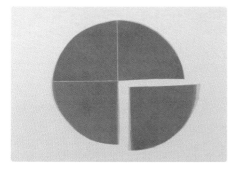

→**1** You will need a template in the shape of ¾ of a circle. To create this template, use a 3-inch (7.6 cm) paper punch to make a disk. Fold the disk in half and crease firmly. Unfold the disk and crease it in the other direction, creating four equally sized quadrants within your circle. Use scissors to remove one quarter of the disk.

→**2** Use the template to mark two disks of paper, as shown.

→**3** Cut out, remove, and discard the quarter circles.

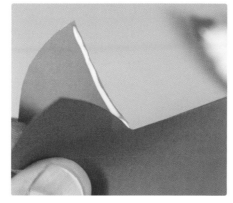

→**4** Apply a very thin line of white glue to one inside edge of one of the paper disks. Place the second disk of paper atop the first so that they align; hold the disks in place until the adhesive has dried completely.

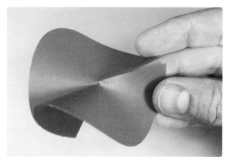

→**5** Gently spread apart the two layers of the circles and press them down over a finger to invert the unglued edges. The shape should resemble a Mobius strip, with the outer surface of one part becoming the inner surface of the other. Once each side has been inverted, adhere together the remaining two straight edges with a very thin line of glue, as in step 4. Hold in place until the adhesive is completely dry.

→**6** When both sets of straight edges have been glued together, the model should look like this.

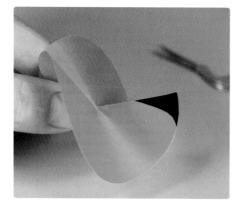 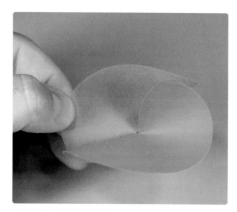 

→ **7** Use small scissors to trim the point of each glued edge, indicated by the shaded area in the photo, for a slightly rounded shape. Repeat on the model's other point.

→ **8** The finished flower should resemble this very pretty, curvy shape.

→ **9** Make a small loop in a short length of floral wire and use hot glue to attach the loop to the middle of the flower. Be sure to angle the stem slightly to mimic the natural appearance of orchids whose blossoms tend to hang off their stems in a slight downward direction.

→ **10** The finished flower. Repeat steps 1 through 9 to create as many blossoms as you want to include in your finished project.

→ **11** Using green floral tape, attach the individual orchid stems to a main wire stem that has itself been wrapped with green floral tape. *Note:* A group of orchid blossoms on a single stem is known as a bract.

→ **12** To make foliage, begin with a few rectangles of green paper in a variety of sizes. Make an incision from each end toward the center, being careful not to cut the rectangle completely in half.

→ **13** Overlap the two flaps at one end of the rectangle and glue them in place.

→ **14** Repeat the process on the other end.

→ **15** Use scissors to trim the paper into a pleasing, oblong shape.

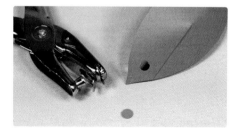

→ **16** Use the ¼-inch (6 mm) hole punch to make a small opening in one end of the leaf. Thread the leaves onto the stem of the orchid, stacking three, four, or more of them loosely around the base of the stalk.

Poinsettia The poinsettia may appear to be a complicated project, but, in fact, it is an easy one. The leaves and red petals ("bracts") are essentially the same shape, though they vary to some degree in size. The leaves and bracts do not need to be cut with precision. The truth is, the more inexact these pieces are, the better and more natural your poinsettia will look. Granted, a realistic poinsettia bush does require a rather large number of pieces, but some simple skills, a little assembly line, and some patience is all that is required for success.

TOOLS SCISSORS OR CRAFT KNIFE ✳ SMALL WIRE CUTTER ✳ HOT GLUE GUN AND GLUE STICKS ✳ QUILLING TOOL OR QUILLING NEEDLE ✳ TWEEZERS (OPTIONAL) **MATERIALS** SHEET OF RED PAPER*, 18 X 24 INCHES (45.7 X 61 CM) ✳ 50 TO 60 PIECES OF 26-GAUGE FLORAL WIRE (CUT INTO 4-INCH [10.2 CM] LENGTHS) ✳ 5 TO 7 PIECES OF FLORAL WIRE (CUT INTO 18-INCH [45.7 CM] LENGTHS) ✳ GREEN FLORAL TAPE ✳ 2 SHEETS OF GREEN PAPER*, 18 X 24 INCHES (45.7 X 61 CM) ✳ SHEET OF YELLOW PAPER, 8 X 10 INCHES (20.3 X 25.4 CM)

I used a red paper with a pique (woven-looking) texture and a green paper with a silk thread running through it. The pique texture gives the red bracts a velvety look, and the thread in the green paper catches the light and adds depth to the finished flower. Do not hesitate to experiment with interesting patterns and textures in your own design. For example, a red and white gingham paper would make your poinsettia look decidedly more modern.

→2 Hot glue about 1 inch (2.5 cm) of a 4-inch (10.2 cm) length of 26-gauge floral wire to the back (convex) side of each bract.

→1 To make each red bract you will need 15 to 24 petal shapes cut in three different sizes (5 to 8 of each size). My shapes are approximately 4 inches (10.2 cm), 3 inches (7.6 cm), and 2 inches (5.1 cm) long. You can vary the size of your bracts as desired. An easy way to create symmetrical shapes is to crease a rectangle of paper down the center, cut out a half profile of your shape, and then unfold the result. You can also use the templates on page 124.

→3 Attach wires to all of your red bracts and allow the glue to fully cool.

→ **4** Carefully make a 90° bend in each wire.

→ **5** To form the stalk of the poinsettia, gather five to seven 18-inch-long (45.7 cm) lengths of floral wire and secure them together using a small piece of green floral tape. Be sure to leave 1½ inches (3.8 cm) of wire unwrapped at the top. *Note:* Do not wrap the entire stalk in tape; just an inch or two should be enough to hold the wires in place.

→ **6** Hold the stalk in one hand and begin placing the smallest red bracts around the stalk in roughly a star-shape. Be sure to leave the 1½ inches (3.8 cm) of the unwrapped stalk protruding above the first row of bracts; the ends of these six wires will form the actual flower at the end of the project.

→ **7** Add the medium-sized bracts followed by the largest bracts.

→ **8** When all of the red bracts are in position, apply just enough floral tape to hold them in place. If the bracts shift as you are wrapping them with tape, you can gently readjust their position by hand.

→ **9** Once the red bracts are in place, repeat steps 1 through 8, using green paper for the leaves. The shape of the leaves is the same as that of the bracts. I suggest two different sizes, 4 inch (10.2 cm) and 3½ inch (8.9 cm), but a single size will also produce an attractive result.

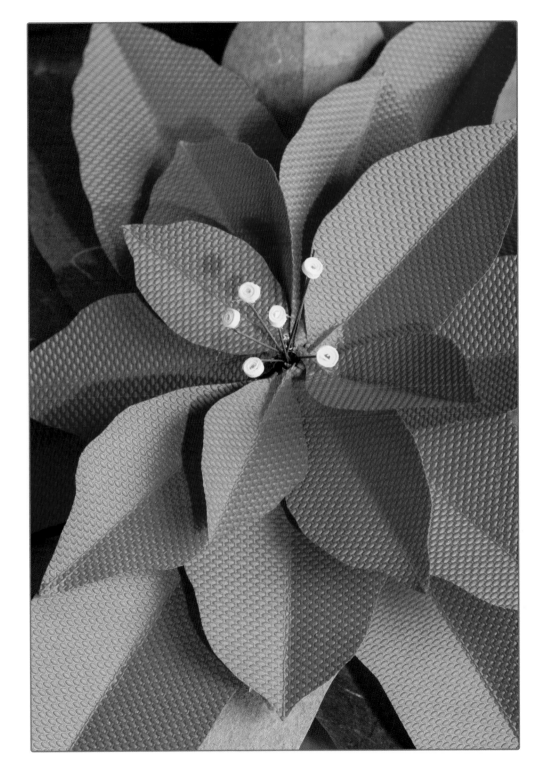

→ **11** Use a quilling tool to create six tiny scrolls of yellow paper. Glue each scroll to prevent it from unraveling.

→ **10** As you did before, hot glue a length of wire to each leaf, bend the wire 90°, and attach groups of five or six leaves every inch (2.5 cm) or so along the stalk until the branch is the desired length. The different-sized leaves can be mixed together at each level, though I prefer to group the smaller leaves toward the bottom to help give the Poinsettia a pleasing shape.

→ **12** To finish the poinsettia, use a tiny dot of hot glue to affix a scroll to each of the wires protruding above the red bracts. Small tweezers may come in handy in this step.

Marigold Some projects require a little intricate cutting while other projects require a little brute force. The humble marigold offers the perfect blend of the two, making it a great project to do with children. Adults can be in charge of cutting out delicate leaves, while children can busy themselves with hand-cutting paper disks (or using paper punches) and crumpling disks of paper in their fists.

TOOLS SCISSORS [OR 2-, 1½-, AND 1-INCH (5.1, 3.8, 2.5 CM) PAPER PUNCHES] ✳ HOT GLUE GUN AND GLUE STICKS
MATERIALS PAPER IN THREE SHADES OF ORANGE ✳ WHITE CRAFT GLUE ✳ FLORAL WIRE ✳ GREEN FLORAL TAPE
✳ GREEN PAPER

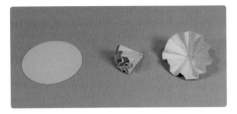

➜1 Punch or cut out three paper disks in three sizes: 2, 1½, and 1 inch (5.1, 3.8, 2.5 cm). Gather the edges of one of the paper disks together into a cone shape. Tightly crumple the paper in your fist. Gently unfold the crumpled paper into a cup shape.

➜2 Repeat step 1 for each of the three differently sized disks of paper.

➜3 Attach the disks to one another using a small amount of white craft glue.

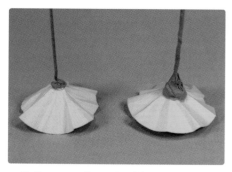

→ **4** Secure a length of floral wire to the back of each marigold using hot glue. Once the glue has cooled, wrap the base of the flower in a length of green floral tape.

→ **5** Fold a 2- x 4- inch (5.1 x 10.2 cm) rectangle of green paper in half lengthwise. Using the pattern on page 123, cut out a pinnate, or feather-like, leaf.

→ **6** Attach the foliage to the stem using a piece of floral tape. Gently shape the leaf as desired.

Carnation   Despite its reputation as a relatively common flower, the carnation has a long history as the "flower of love," beloved both for its beautiful ruffled appearance and its lovely clove scent. In this version you will use a decidedly common and familiar material to create a bouquet of subtle and uncommon beauty.

TOOLS SMALL PAINTBRUSH ✱ NEEDLE-NOSE PLIERS ✱ SCISSORS OR CRAFT KNIFE ✱ HOT GLUE GUN AND GLUE STICKS **MATERIALS** FLUTED COFFEE FILTERS ✱ RED PAINT ✱ GREEN FLORAL WIRE ✱ GREEN FLORAL TAPE

➜**1** Begin by grasping the center of a fluted coffee filter, as shown.

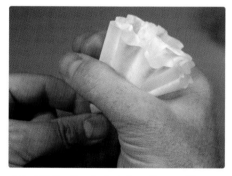

➜**2** While firmly holding the coffee filter in one hand, use your other hand to draw the edges of the filter together into a cone-shape.

➜**3** Tightly twist the pointed end about one half of the way up the filter. Be careful not to compress or crush the fluted ends.

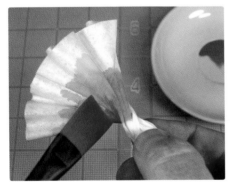

→ **4** Use a small brush to apply a modest daub of watercolor to one side of the twisted filter, leaving the other side unpainted.

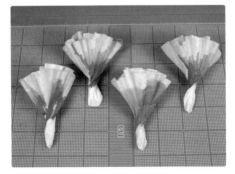

→ **5** Repeat steps 1 through 4 until you have four identical components.

→ **6** Gather together all four components, being careful to position the painted surfaces inward and the unpainted surfaces outward. Bind them together using pliers and a small length of wire.

→ **7** Once the components are securely attached to one another, trim off any excess portion of the stem.

→ **8** Apply a small bead of hot glue to the base of the flower.

→ **9** Insert a length of green floral wire and hold it in position until the glue is completely dry.

→ **10** Tightly wrap the base of the flower and the wire stem with green floral tape.

→ **11 VARIATION:** As shown, flowers can be left completely white. Also, a variety of sizes can be achieved by using four, three, or two components for each blossom.

Poppy   In this project, the crinkly characteristic of glassine (a thin, strong, and inexpensive paper, similar to tissue paper but with more body) is used to capture the delicate crepe-like texture of poppies. The crumpled paper is surprisingly receptive to being shaped by hand. Glassine is available in many jewel tones, and the finished flower, when placed within reach of the afternoon sun, will glow and shimmer in the most appealing way.

TOOLS SCISSORS OR CRAFT KNIFE ✳ HOT GLUE GUN AND GLUE STICKS **MATERIALS** RED GLASSINE PAPER*, TWO 6½- INCH (16.5 CM) DISKS PER FLOWER ✳ WHITE CRAFT GLUE ✳ STRIP OF PALE GREEN PAPER ✳ STRIP OF BLACK PAPER ✳ WHITE CORRECTION LIQUID (OR WHITE PAINT) ✳ FLORAL WIRE ✳ GREEN FLORAL TAPE

Glassine is a wonderful paper to work with as it is both thin and strong, and responds well to crumpling and creasing. It is available at many art supply stores and is very inexpensive.

→**1** Cut two 6½ inch (16.5 cm) circles out of red glassine. Roughly divide each circle in thirds by making a small, tapered cut, as shown (or see the template on page 126).

→**2** Place a finger in the middle of a disk and press it into the fist of your other hand, bringing the edges of the disk together and creating a cup shape.

→**3** Tightly and repeatedly, squeeze the paper in your fist to create as many creases as possible.

→**4** Carefully open the disk, turn it inside out, and recollapse it into a cup shape as in step 2, and crease again.

→ **7** Use scissors to separate the disk into three separate sections, cutting it apart at the notches created in step 1. Repeat steps 2 through 7 for the second disk.

→ **8** Use scissors to make a small ½-inch (1.3 cm) incision in the pointed tip of each petal.

→ **5** Repeat step 3, squeezing the paper in your fist for additional creases. The result should be a piece of paper that has many sharp creases radiating from the center of the disk.

→ **6** Carefully open the paper about halfway, being careful not to flatten it completely in the process.

→ **9** Add a small dot of white craft glue to one side of the incision.

→ 10 Fold the two sides of the incision together at a 90° angle and hold in place until the glue dries.

→ 11 The result will be a slightly curved petal with a flat bottom.

→ 12 Repeat with the remaining five petals.

→ 13 Attach two petals to each other by their centers with a dot of white craft glue. Slightly overlap the edges of the first and second petals.

→ 14 Attach the third petal, overlapping its edges slightly with the previous two petals.

→ **15** Continue gluing the remaining three petals around the outside of the first three until you have a fully formed blossom.

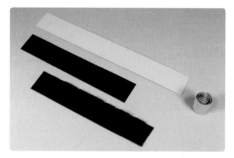

→ **16** To create the center of the poppy, make a loose scroll using a 1 x 5 ½-inch (2.5 x 14 cm) strip of pale green paper. Use a strip of black paper and a pair of scissors to create a strip of fringed paper.

→ **17** Glue the fringed black paper around the green scroll. Be sure to position the black paper so that

the fringe extends above the top of the scroll. Shape the fringe with your fingers.

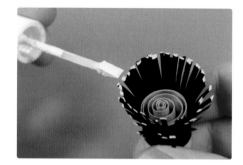

→ **18** Use white correction fluid or a small amount of white paint to apply highlights to the ends of the fringe.

→ **19** Attach the flower center to the middle of the glassine petals with a generous dot of hot glue. Hold in place until dry. Poppy leaves are elaborately shaped and can be time consuming to create. Luckily, these flowers are bold enough to stand on their own without added foliage.

→ **20** To finish, hot glue a sinuous stem to the bottom of the flower and arrange in groups of three or five stems.

Dogwood   Many legends and meanings are associated with the dog-wood tree. However, regardless of this flower lore, there are few pleasures as simple and rewarding as sitting beneath its branches on a spring day. Whether the blossoms are white, white with pink tips, or fully pink, the beautiful effect of flowers and foliage dappled with sunlight is one of the most eagerly awaited signs that winter is finally past. Lovely as they are, dogwood blossoms are fleeting. With this project you can capture and keep them for far longer than is possible with real dogwood.

TOOLS WIRE CUTTERS * PLIERS * MARKER * SCISSORS OR CRAFT KNIFE * PAINTBRUSH * HOT GLUE GUN AND GLUE STICKS * BUTTER KNIFE **MATERIALS** WIRE HANGER * ALUMINUM FOIL * BROWN FLORAL TAPE * WHITE COFFEE FILTERS (FLUTED) * PINK OR RED WATERCOLOR PAINT * MUSTARD SEEDS (WHOLE) * DARK GREEN PAPER*

Crinkled or crepe papers have nice textures, but any dark green paper will suffice for the foliage.

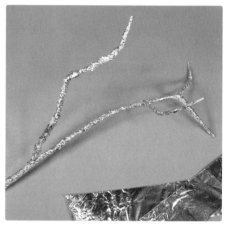

➜ **3** Once the wire has been roughly shaped into a branch, wrap the entire armature with narrow strips of aluminum foil to create a more convincing twig-like shape.

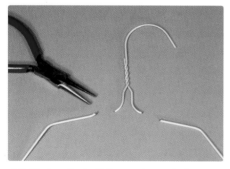

➜ **1** To begin building a branch for dogwood blossoms, use a wire cutter to remove the hook from a wire hanger.

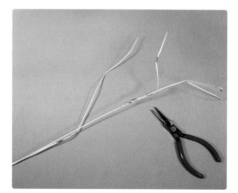

➜ **2** Use pliers to bend the wire into a pleasing, branch-like shape. The hanger's hook, removed in step 1, can be used to augment the armature by forming it into a small branch and attaching it with pliers.

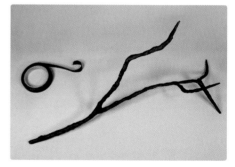

➜ **4** Tightly wrap the entire branch with brown floral tape.

→ 5 For the blossoms, white coffee filters provide the perfect material. Flatten the pleated filter and fold it in half. Then fold it again, into quarters, and once more into a one-eighth wedge. Firmly press all of the creases using your finger.

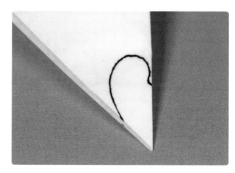

→ 6 Mark a sort of half-heart shape onto the filter (or use the template on page 123), making sure a single crease runs along the right-hand side of the model. Cut out the shape.

TIP: It might help to glance ahead a few steps to acquaint yourself with what the final shape should look like.

→ 7 Notice the thin shape that is left behind on the filter after you have removed the petals. This shape confirms that your blossom has the distinguishing notch of the dogwood flower on the tip of each petal.

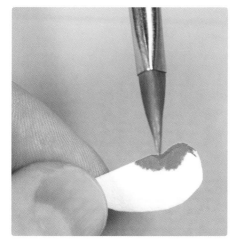

→ 8 Without unfolding the petal, daub a small amount of bright pink watercolor onto the notched area. The color will be absorbed by the porous material.

→ 9 Allow the watercolor to dry, then unfold the model. Recrease the flower so that creases that run through the centers of the flowers are convex (mountain folded) and the creases between the petals are concave (valley folded).

→ 10 With the flower positioned as in step 9, grip a petal between the thumb and forefinger of each of your hands. Pinch the petals between your fingers while gently pressing both hands toward the center of the flower. This action is less one of creasing and more one of crumpling. Best results will be achieved by making sure the pink petal tips remain flat on your work surface while you pinch the paper together. Repeat this maneuver with the remaining two petals of the flower.

→ **11** The resulting blossom should look like this. Notice that the petals remain flat against the work surface but the creases have been pressed into upstanding pleats. This is the back of the flower.

→ **12** Gently turn the flower over. You should now see small channels running down the center of each petal.

→ **13** Leaves are created by folding a 1- x 2- inch (2.5 x 5.1 cm) piece of paper in half lengthwise, and cutting out a simple oval-shape with a small tab at one end.

→ **14** Attach leaves in groups of two, three, or four by applying a dot of hot glue beneath each tab.

→ **15** Attach the flower to the leaves by placing it atop a generous dot of hot glue. Gently hold the flower until the glue dries.

→ **16** Dogwood blossoms have small, seed-like clusters at their centers. An easy way to replicate these clusters is to place a ¼- to ½- inch-diameter (6 mm to 1.3 cm) dot of hot glue onto a heat-safe work surface. While the glue is still hot, pour a teaspoon of whole mustard seeds over it. The seeds will adhere to the glue as it dries. When the glue has hardened, gently brush away any loose seeds that remain and use the blade of a butter knife to pry the piece from your work surface.

→ **17** Hot glue the mustard-seed center to the flower.

→ **18** Attach the completed flower and foliage to the branch with hot glue. Hold the components in place until the glue dries.

Calla Lily   The calla lily has been many things to many people: a symbol of purity to some, a symbol of lust to others. Katherine Hepburn famously dubbed it "a strange flower; suitable to any occasion." The question is: How do you create such a bold, sensual, and asymmetrical blossom using only a sheet of flat paper? The solution turns out to be so simple you may want to make a dozen or more of these dramatic beauties.

TOOLS SCISSORS OR CRAFT KNIFE ✳ HOT GLUE GUN AND GLUE STICKS ✳ 2-INCH (5.1 CM) PAPER PUNCH ✳ BAMBOO SKEWER **MATERIALS** YELLOW, GREEN, AND ORANGE TRANSLUCENT PAPER ✳ WHITE CRAFT GLUE ✳ FLORAL WIRE ✳ GREEN FLORAL TAPE

➜**1** Fold a 6 x 4½-inch (15.2 x 11.4 cm) sheet of yellow, translucent paper in half to create a 3 x 4½-inch (7.6 x 11.4 cm) double sheet, and cut from it the shape shown.

TIP: There is a template on page 124, but I encourage you to draw the design by hand to ensure variation in each flower.

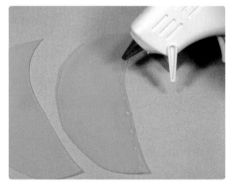

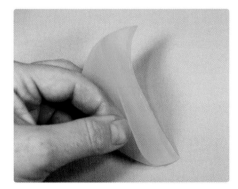

➜**2** Apply a bead of hot glue along the inside edge (the mostly straight edge) of one piece. Align the second piece over the first and press firmly to ensure a strong bond. Allow to dry before proceeding.

➜**3** The resulting piece will consist of two gently curved flaps that are affixed to each other by a line of glue.

➜**4** Gently fold the non-glued edges of the pieces inward, creating a cone shape.

→ **5** Use a 2-inch (5.1 cm) paper punch to create a disk of green paper.

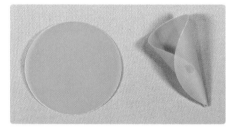

→ **6** As with the yellow flower, create a cone by folding two edges inward and affixing with hot glue.

→ **7** Use a small dot of hot glue to affix the green cone shape to the base of the yellow flower. Hold the piece in place until the glue is dry.

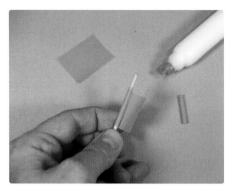

→ **8** To create a tight orange tube, wind a 1½ x 1-inch (3.8 x 2.5 cm) rectangle of orange paper around a bamboo skewer (or other thin dowel) and secure with white craft glue. Remove the dowel and allow the glue to dry.

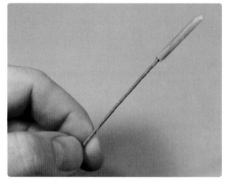

→ **9** To form the stem, add a small amount of hot glue to one end of the orange tube and insert a piece of green floral wire.

TIP: I used fabric-covered wire but if using plain wire, be sure to wrap it with green floral tape before attaching it to the orange tube in step 9.

→ **10** Apply a dot of hot glue to the base of the orange tube where it meets the wire, then carefully insert the wire into the blossom and pull it through until the orange tube is firmly seated at the base. Carefully position the stem, flower, and flower center and hold in place until the hot glue dries.

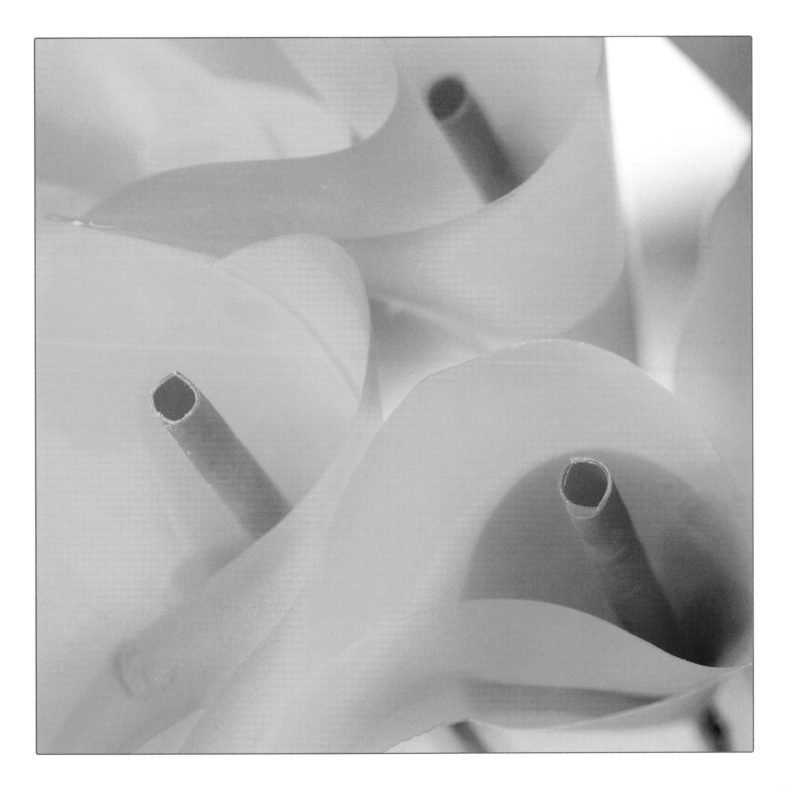

Tiger Lily   Folklore claims that tiger lilies represent wealth. While I cannot attest to this moneyed connection, I know that for me they have always heralded those late summer days when the air is warm, the nights are clear, and the crickets are at their most talkative.

TOOLS SCISSORS OR CRAFT KNIFE ✳ STRAIGHTEDGE ✳ STYLUS OR BONE FOLDER ✳ BLACK FELT-TIP MARKER ✳ PENCIL OR SMALL DOWEL **MATERIALS** FLOWER TEMPLATE ✳ ORANGE PAPER ✳ WHITE CRAFT GLUE ✳ WHITE PAPER ✳ GREEN PAPER ✳ FLORAL WIRE ✳ GREEN FLORAL TAPE

→**1** Use the templates on pages 128 and 129 to create two halves of a six-pointed flower shape.

→**2** Fold one of the flower halves down the center of each petal. The necessary creases are indicated on the left; the folded piece is shown on the right. Using a straightedge as a guide, you can pre-create these lines by drawing a stylus or bone folder firmly across the paper before folding it. Scoring the paper in this manner will ensure that it creases sharply.

→**3** Fold the other flower half *between* the petals rather than down their centers. Again, the necessary creases are indicated at left; the folded piece is shown at right.

TIP: It is easiest to add the lily's dot pattern along each petal at this step. I have forgone the dots in the photos to keep the assembly of the pieces clearer. Use a felt-tip marker and refer to the main project photo for dot placement.

→**4** Lay the creased piece from step 3 on the table in front of you, and then fold and position the creased piece from step 2 on top of it. Glue the pieces in place as shown, using white craft glue. Allow to dry before proceeding.

→ **5** Rotate the flower so you are now looking at the back of it. Fold the petals of the bottom piece up onto the sides of the top piece and glue them in place. Allow the glue to dry before proceeding.

→ **6** Once the two pieces have been affixed to one another, the flower should look like this.

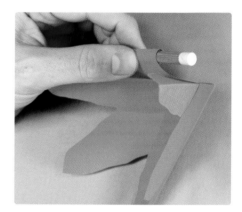

→ **7** Gently roll each petal around the shaft of a pencil or a dowel to curl. Repeat for all six petals.

→ **8** Once all petals have been curled, the flower should look like this.

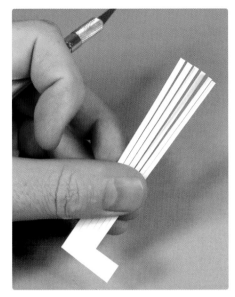

→ **9** Using a craft knife or scissors, create a small, fringed piece of white paper with a tiny tail (see the template on page 127). This will form the stamen. If you would like, daub the end of each tiny strip with a black marker to suggest a little pollen pod.

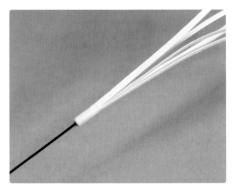

→ **10** Beginning with the tiny tail, roll the fringed paper strip tightly into a scroll and hot glue it to the end of a length of floral wire.

→ **11** Add a dot of hot glue to the bottom of the stamen and then insert the end of the floral wire through the center of the flower. Grasp the wire where it comes out the bottom of the flower and pull it through until the stamen is firmly seated in the cup of the flower. Center the stamen in your blossom and hold in place until the glue is dry.

→ **12** Wrap the stem with green floral wire. Use the leaf template on page 127 to make the leaves from green paper. Affix them to the stem using floral tape.

Daffodil   The poet William Wordsworth called them "jocund," but to many people, these lovely flowers are not merely cheerful, they are the very harbingers of spring. The key to this model is a cleverly folded piece of paper that when trimmed just so, produces a beautiful three-petal shape. A pair of these shapes, crowned with a corona of crumpled paper, is surprisingly realistic looking and unquestioningly charming.

TOOLS 3-INCH (7.6 CM) PAPER PUNCH ✳ PENCIL ✳ 2-INCH (5.1 CM) PAPER PUNCH ✳ SCISSORS OR CRAFT KNIFE ✳ HOT GLUE GUN AND GLUE STICKS **MATERIALS** YELLOW TRANSLUCENT PAPER* ✳ ORANGE TRANSLUCENT PAPER* ✳ GREEN FLORAL WIRE ✳ BROWN OR BEIGE TISSUE PAPER ✳ GREEN FLORAL TAPE ✳ GREEN PAPER

Translucent paper is ideal, but solid papers work as well.

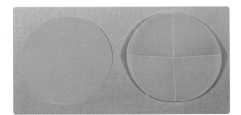

➜ **1** The key to this design is an equilateral triangle. You can easily create a template in a few short steps. Begin by folding a 3-inch (7.6 cm) disk of paper into four equal quadrants, as shown.

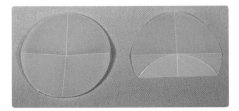

➜ **2** Fold the bottom up to the center point where the two creases intersect, as shown. This is the base of the triangle.

➜ **3** The remaining sides of the triangle will be folded on the two dotted lines, which are illustrated.

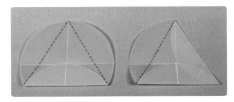

➜ **4** Fold the right side of the model in toward the center of the disk, and crease.

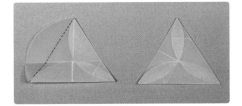

➜ **5** Fold the left side of the model in toward the center of the disk, and crease. The resulting triangle can now be used as a template for creating a daffodil.

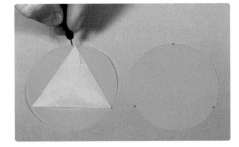

➜ **6** Use the triangle template and a pencil (not a pen, as is shown) to lightly mark three points on a 3-inch (7.6 cm) disk of yellow paper. I used a pen so that the dots would be easy to see in the photo. The pencil marks will be later erased.

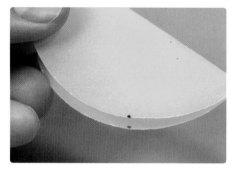

→ **7** Align any two dots on the disk and firmly fold the paper in half.

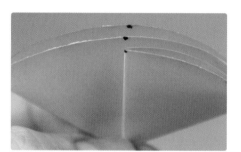

→ **8** With the disk still folded in half, align the remaining dot (the third dot) with the other two and crease in place.

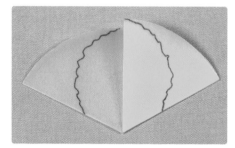

→ **9** With the three dots on the disk aligned, use a pencil to lightly sketch a petal shape or use the template on page 123.

TIP: A wavy line will give the flower petals a natural, ruffled look.

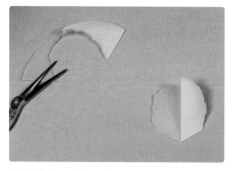

→ **10** Cut out the shape.

→ **11** Carefully unfold the petals. (***Note:*** Because of the way the paper was folded in step 8, two petals will have concave creases and one will have a convex crease. Refold so that all three petals are creased in the same direction.) Repeat steps 1 through 10 to make a second set of petals.

→ **12** Position the two sets of petals as pictured, and affix them with at their centers with a dot of hot glue.

→ **13** To create the daffodil's corona, begin with a 2-inch (5.1 cm) disk of orange translucent paper and a pencil.

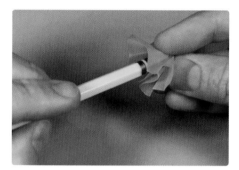

→ **14** Using the end of a pencil as a form, crumple the edges of the paper disk upward.

→ **15** Press firmly until the paper is tightly crumpled into place.

→ 16 Once the paper has been well creased, gently spread the edges a little bit to form a ruffled cup.

→ 17 Use a small dot of hot glue to affix the crumpled paper to the center of the yellow petals.

→ 18 Form a loop at the end of a length of floral wire and hot glue it to the bottom of the flower. Hold the stem in place until the glue dries.

→ 19 Thread a 2-inch (5.1 cm) square of brown or beige tissue paper onto the wire stem.

→ 20 Crumple and twist the tissue paper to form the spathe (a small leaf-like sheath that encloses the underside of a daffodil flower). The spathe is an important detail that is not only attractive but will also hide from view the area where the stem is glued to the base of the flower. Finish the flower by wrapping the stem and the base of the spathe with a length of dark green floral tape. Daffodil stems usually bend at a slight angle just below the spathe, so be sure to shape your stem accordingly. Add a few spear-shaped leaves using the Tiger Lily Leaf template found on page 127.

Sunflower   Sunflowers range in size from a few inches wide to more than a foot (30.5 cm) across. Most varieties sport bright yellow flowers with prominent, dark centers. Best of all, there is hardly a flower more readily associated with sheer happiness. This design mimics not only the exuberance of the real flowers but also the hearty stems and foliage that give these guardians of the garden so much personality.

TOOLS SCISSORS AND CRAFT KNIFE ✳ STRAIGHTEDGE ✳ HOT GLUE GUN AND GLUE STICKS ✳ BLACK MARKER ✳ ⅝-INCH (1.6 CM) PAPER PUNCH **MATERIALS** ½- X 38-INCH (1.3 X 96.5 CM) STRIP OF CORRUGATED CARDBOARD ✳ YELLOW TRANSLUCENT PAPER ✳ GREEN PAPER ✳ CARDBOARD TUBE (FROM A PANTS HANGER) ✳ GREEN FLORAL TAPE

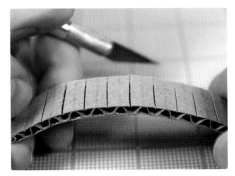

→**1** The sunflower is built from the center outward. Create a ½- x 38-inch (1.3 x 96.5 cm) strip of corrugated cardboard. (**Note:** be sure to cut the cardboard so that the fluting, or corrugation, inside is visible along the length of the strip.) Use a craft knife to incise lines between each of the flutes on one side; this will allow the cardboard to be rolled smoothly into a round shape without puckering or buckling.

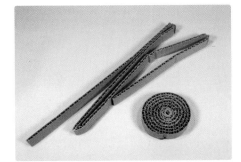

→**2** Roll the strip with the incised surface facing inward and the uncut surface facing outward. Secure the end of the scrolled cardboard with a generous amount of hot glue, and hold in place until the glue has dried.

→**3** Color the face of the disk using a wide black marker.

→**4** When the ink from the marker is dry, gently push the center of the disk upward to create a slightly domed shape.

→**5** Apply hot glue in an "X" across the back of the disk to hold the domed shape in place.

→ **6** To make the petals, accordion-fold a 3 x 2½-inch (7.6 x 6.4 cm) rectangle into six equal sections.

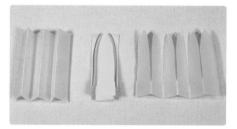

→ **7** Compress the accordion and carefully trim most of the way (though not all of the way) down each side, rounding one end to create a petal shape (see page 127 for a template). When unfolded you should have six individual sunflower petals that are still connected at the bottom.

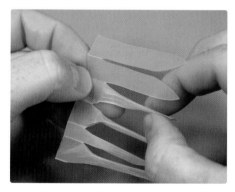

→ **8** Firmly crinkle and crease each petal, then smooth it out again.

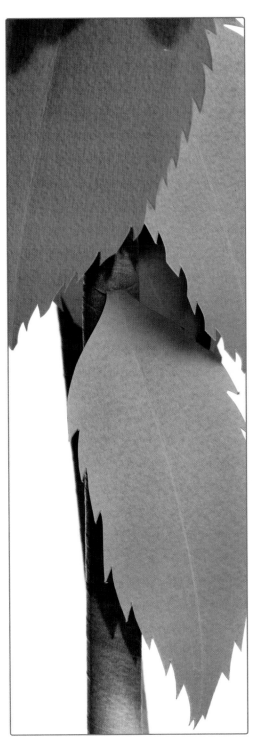

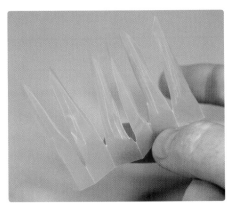

→ **9** When finished, your petals should look like this. For a full-size sunflower, you will need to repeat steps 6 through 8 eight to 10 times.

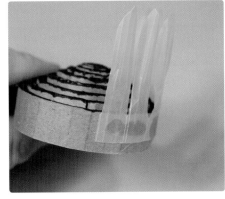

→ **10** Attach the flower petals to the side of the cardboard disk using hot glue.

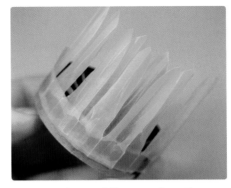

→ **11** Continue adding petal sections, being sure to slightly overlap each new section with the previous section.

TIP: This overlap is important if your sunflower is to look natural. Petal sections that are no longer than three inches (7.6 cm) will not create the desired effect. As well, longer strips of petals are difficult to work with when hot gluing.

→ **12** After applying two rows of petal sections around the cardboard center, the flower should look like this.

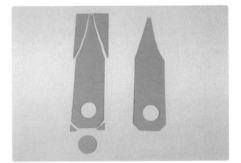

→ **13** To form the area underneath the flower, you will need nine strips of 1- x 6-inch (2.5 x 15.2 cm) green paper. A template can be found on page 127. Trim the bottom corners of each strip and taper the top edges. Finally, use a ⅝-inch (1.6 cm) paper punch to make a round opening near one end.

→ 14 Attach a stem to your sunflower, (a cardboard tube from a wire hanger works very well) using a generous amount of hot glue. One by one, thread the green strips onto the stem and attach them to the right side of the cardboard disk (directly on top of the yellow petals) using a dot of hot glue.

TIP: You may wish to bend the cardboard stem to give shape to your sunflower, but if you do, be sure to add a little hot glue to the bent area in order to strengthen it.

→ 15 When all of the green strips are glued in place, wrap the stem with green floral tape.

→ 16 Bend each green strip downward, and pinch to shape.

→ 17 Open out all of the yellow petals and press them into shape by creasing the base of each petal.

→ 18 Using the photo above as a reference, cut out large, geen leaves and attach them to the sunflower's stalk with green floral tape.

Inspiration

There are many ways you can display and share your paper blooms; the possibilities extend far beyond arranging a few stems in a vase. Here are a few ideas to inspire your own creations.

TEMPLATES

(actual size)

Dahlia Leaf

Pumpkin Leaf

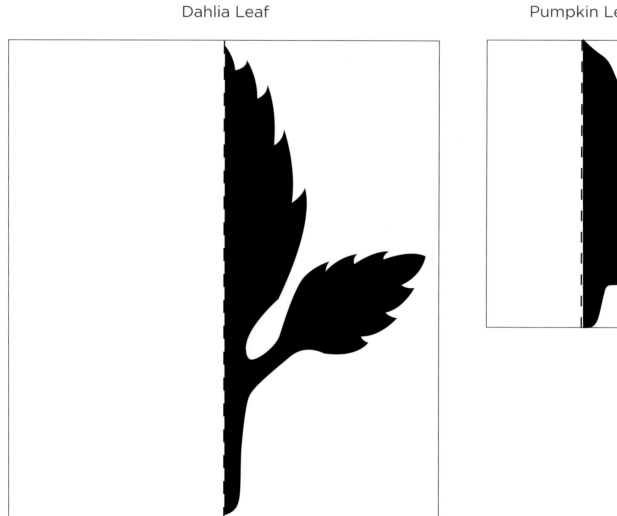

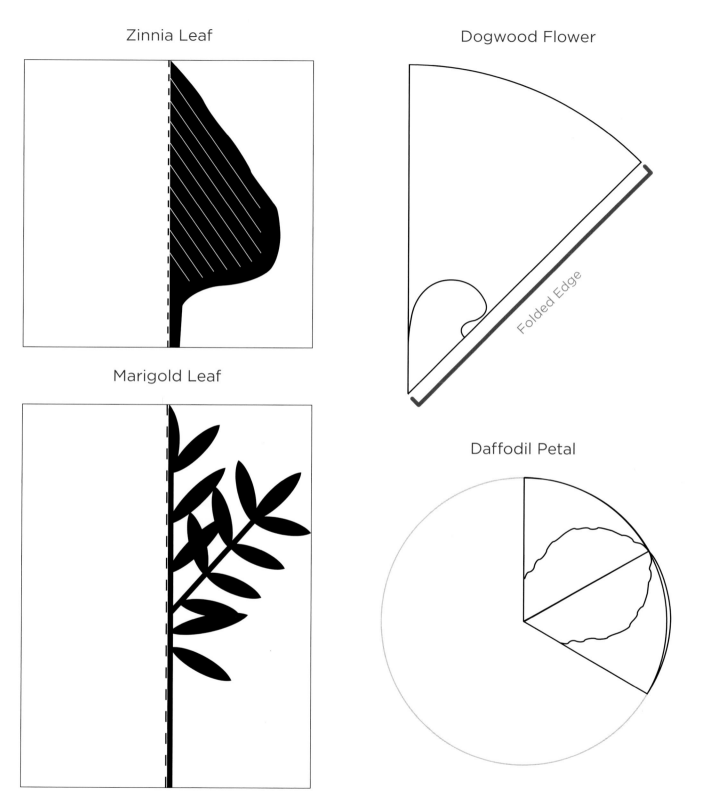

Zinnia Leaf

Dogwood Flower

Folded Edge

Marigold Leaf

Daffodil Petal

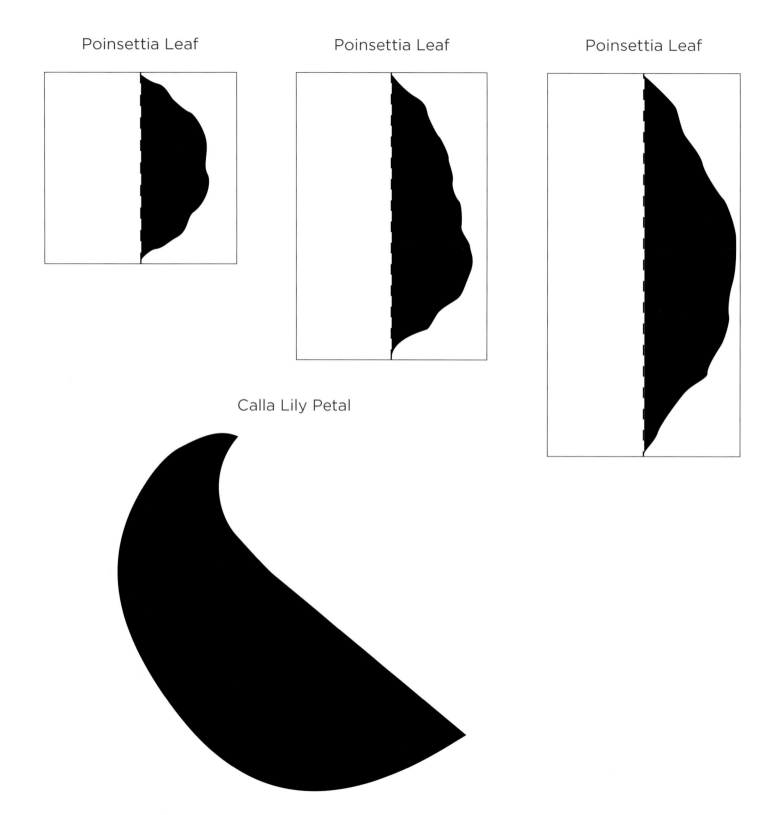

Poinsettia Leaf

Poinsettia Leaf

Poinsettia Leaf

Calla Lily Petal

English Rose Flower

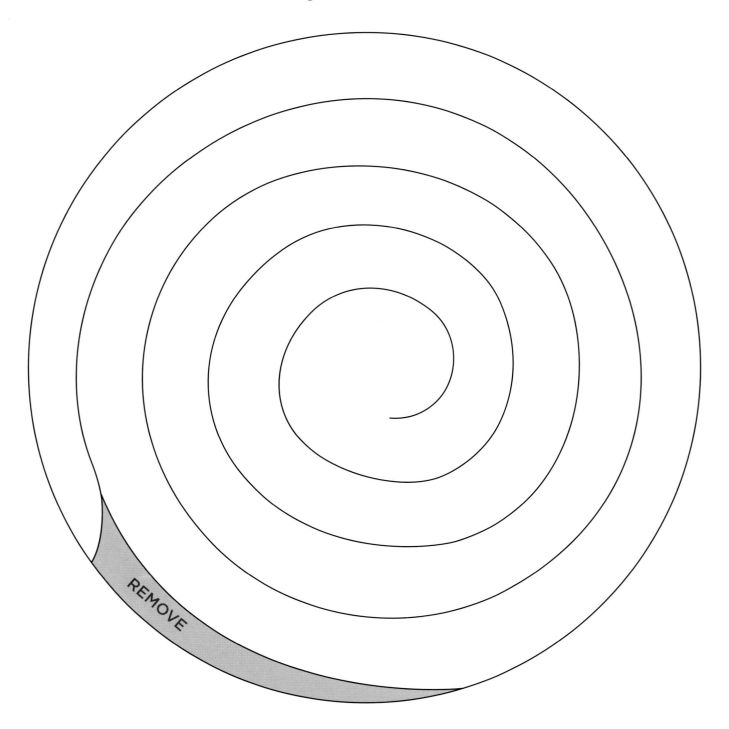

REMOVE

Poppy Flower

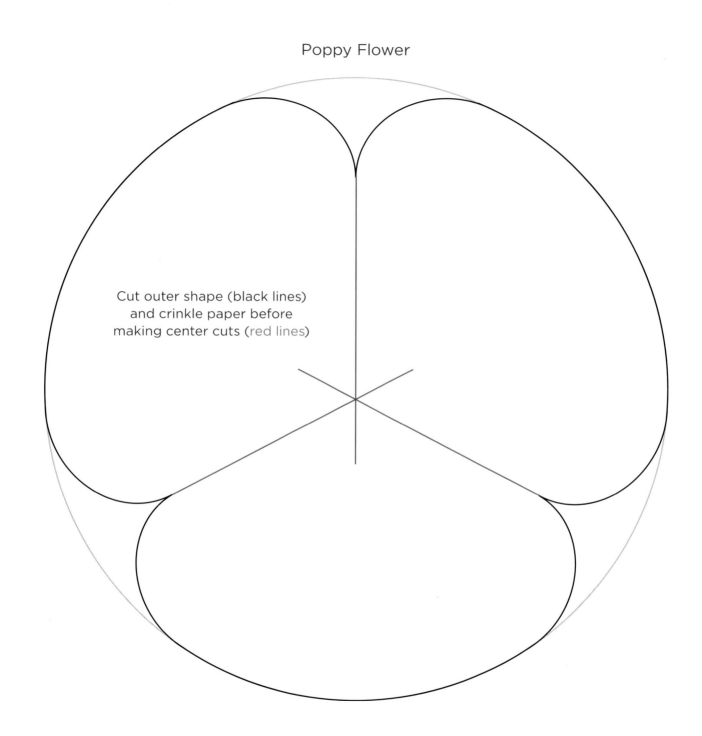

Cut outer shape (black lines)
and crinkle paper before
making center cuts (red lines)

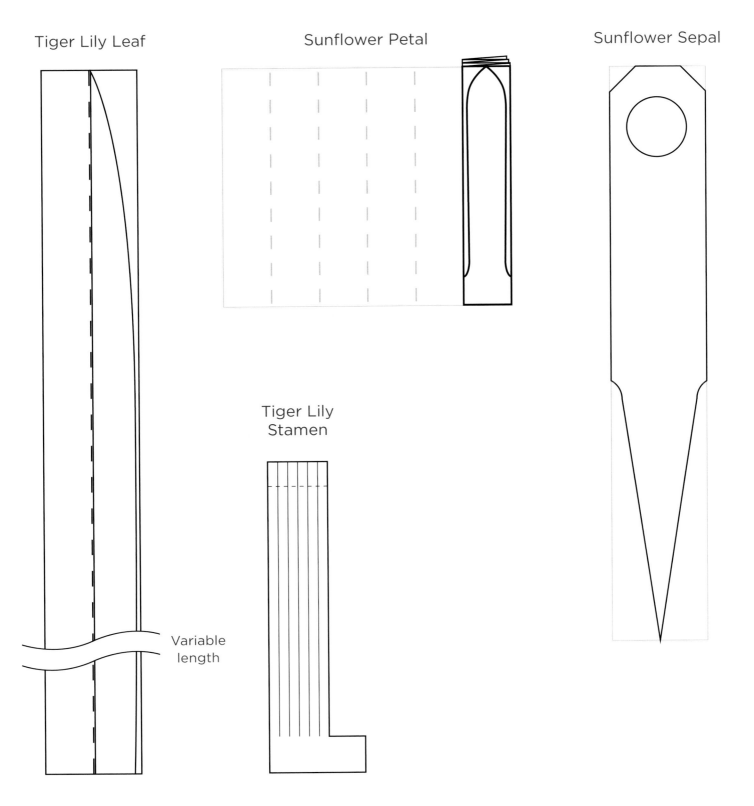

Tiger Lily Leaf

Sunflower Petal

Sunflower Sepal

Variable length

Tiger Lily Stamen

Tiger Lily Flower (Part 1)

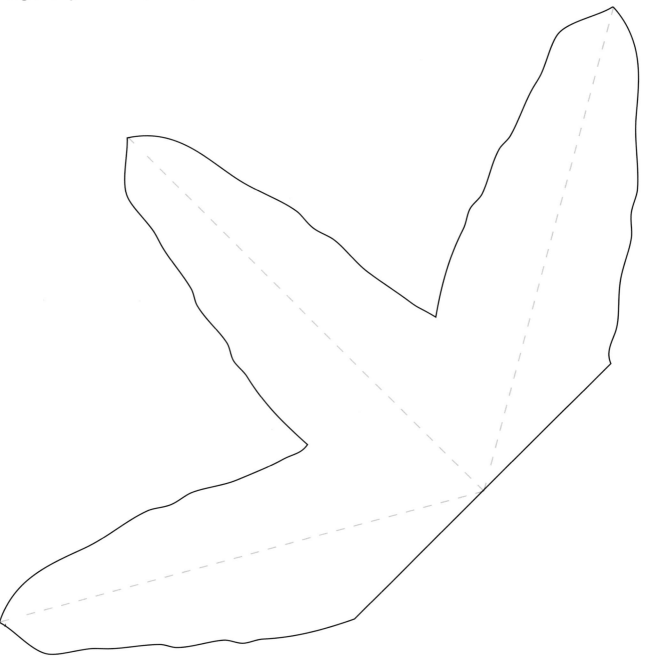

Tiger Lily Flower (Part 2)

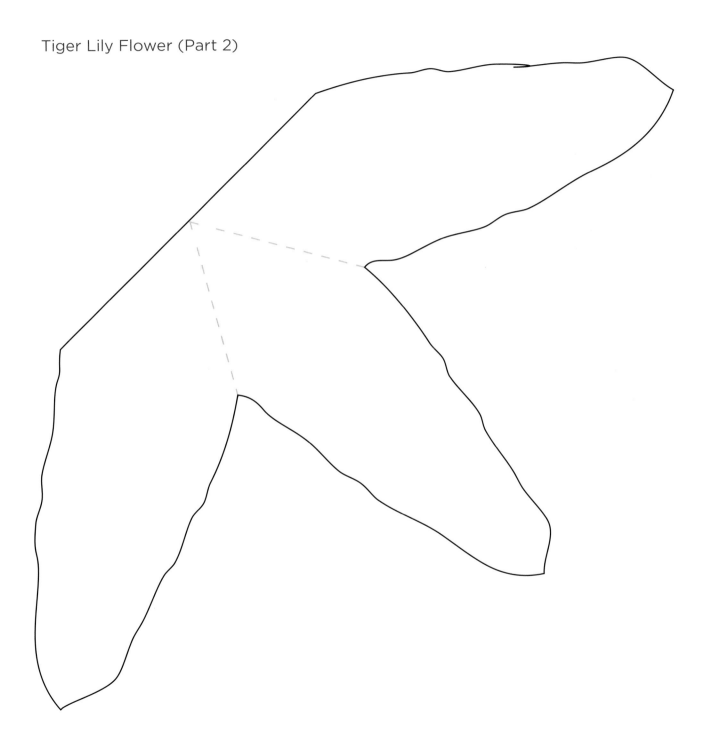

ACKNOWLEDGMENTS

It is curious that my name should occupy the place of honor as author of this book. In any fair world, a long list of other names would precede mine, since I was assisted at every turn by many talented (and tirelessly supportive) people, all of whom put in at least as much effort as I. Of those many, I would, in particular, like to offer special thanks to the following:

Pamela Horn, Editorial Director of Sterling Innovation, who invited me to bring a box of paper scraps into her office one day and who, in an act of will as much as vision, conjured up this book in its original form.

David Aldera, Kathy Hyde, Kelly Hunt, and the staff in the paper department at New York Central Art Supply, who have spent years teaching me three important lessons: 1) "white" refers to a hundred different colors, 2) expensive paper is worth every penny, and 3) indecisive customers go to the back of the line.

David Schofield, Michaela Murphy, and Diane Gilleland—craft heroes all—who shared with me their way of making things, encouraged me to make things of my own, suggested ways to make things better, and then patted me on the back and told me, "you did it all yourself."

Linda Kopp, Kristi Pfeffer, and Nicole McConville, my team at Lark Crafts, who were equal parts midwives, drill sergeants, and fairy godmothers to this project. Were it not for their experience, expertise, insight, and skill at herding cats you would not now be holding this book.

Most importantly, Albert Wilcox, who taught me it takes a great deal of time, patience, and love to grow a garden.

ABOUT THE AUTHOR

Jeffery Rudell is a graphic designer and professional paper artist who specializes in custom window displays and paper props for corporate and private clients. He is the author of several books on paper crafts and a series of popular online craft tutorials.

He is also a noted spoken-word storyteller and writer whose work has been heard on on NPR's *All Things Considered*, performed at the New York Public Library, and featured on the National Storytelling Tour. He lives in New York City.

Editor
Linda Kopp

Art Director
Kristi Pfeffer

Photographers
Stewart O'Shields

Step-By-Step Photographer
Jeffery Rudell

Cover Designer
Kristi Pfeffer

Editorial Assistance
Alex Alexi

INDEX